Meanings of Old Age and Aging in the Tradition of India

Editors

Dr Shrinivas Tilak

Dr Yashwant Pathak

Publisher

Hindu Swayamsevak Sangh, USA Inc.

http://www.hssus.org

Publisher:
Hindu Swayamsevak Sangh USA Inc. (HSS)
121 Hawthorne Court
Rockaway, NJ 07866
www.hssus.org

E-mail: info@hssus.org

Typesetter: Abhimanyu Gupta
Cover Designers: Gauri Manglik, Abhimanyu Gupta

Printed in the United States of America

Table of Contents

INTRODUCTION [SHRINIVAS TILAK] ... 1

GERONTOPHILIA, GERONTOPHOBIA, AND GERONTOCRACY IN THE TRADITION OF INDIA ... 2
BUDDHIST CRITIQUE OF OLD AGE (GERONTOPHOBIA) ... 3
COMPROMISE IN THE DHARMAŚĀSTRAS (GERONTOCRACY) ... 3
OLD AGE AND THE ELDERLY: A PERSPECTIVE FROM GERONTOLOGY ... 6

AGE SENSITIVE GRADING OF LIFE SPAN IN THE ĀŚRAMA MODEL [SHRINIVAS TILAK] ... 12

INTRODUCTION ... 12
GRADING ON THE BASIS OF AGE ... 13
LIFE COURSE: A CULTURAL PERSPECTIVE ... 14
MEANINGFUL ACTION ... 14
AGE SENSITIVE DUTIES ... 15
ĀŚRAMADHARMA ... 17
CONCLUDING REMARKS ... 17
SIX ESSENTIAL CONSTITUENTS ... 18

CARING FOR THE AGED IN ĀYURVEDA: METAPHYSICAL, SEMIOTIC, AND ETHICAL CONSIDERATIONS [SHRINIVAS TILAK] ... 19

ETHICS OF ELDERLY HEALTHCARE ... 19
TYPICAL ATTITUDES TOWARD OLD AGE AND AGING ... 20
HEALTHCARE IN ĀYURVEDA ... 21
NURSING AND CARING ACTION: METAPHYSICAL CONSIDERATIONS ... 22
NURSING AND CARING ACTION: SEMIOTIC CONSIDERATIONS ... 24
SEMIOSIS OF OLD AGE ... 25
NURSING AND CARING ACTION: ETHICAL CONSIDERATIONS ... 29
INTERACTION BETWEEN ETHICS AND MEDICINE ... 33
CARE AND ITS DELIVERY (*ŚUŚRUṢĀ*) ... 34
DELIVERING HEALTH CARE ... 35
ETHICAL DILEMMA OF THE ELDERLY PATIENT ... 36
RIGHT TO HEALTHCARE IN ĀYURVEDA ... 38
SCOPE FOR CROSS-CULTURAL RESEARCH ... 40
COMPARATIVE ETHICS OF HEALTHCARE ... 42

DEPICTIONS OF OLD AGE IN SANSKRIT LITERATURE [SHRINIVAS TILAK] ... 45

INTRODUCTION ... 45
SEMANTIC DOMAIN OF AGE ... 46
LANGUAGE AND MEANING IN THE INDIAN TRADITION ... 50
MODES OF EXPRESSING AGE ... 55
NOMINAL COMPOSITION ... 56
NOMINAL COMPOSITION BUILT ON NUMERAL BASE ... 61
NOMINAL COMPOSITION IN FORMALIZED LISTS ... 63
COLOUR VOCABULARY ... 64

Optative mood 67
Assonance 69

VIGNETTES OF OLD AGE IN AŚVAGHOṢA'S BUDDHACARITA AND SAUNDARANANDA [SHRINIVAS TILAK] 75

Aśvaghoṣa 75
Buddhacarita 76
Siddhārtha 77
Exposure to diseases, aging, and death 77
Promoting renunciation (nivṛtti) 79
Saundarananda 83
Goal of human life 87
Concluding remarks 89

MODEL OF SUCCESSFUL AGING: THE CASE OF DHṚTARĀṢṬRA [SHRINIVAS TILAK] 92

Integrating old age and death into life 92
Life and career of Dhṛtarāṣṭra: reconciling fate with human initiative93
Karma and the stages of life model 94
Aging as career: theory of differential disengagement 96
Significant events in Dhṛtarāṣṭra's career 98
Discussion 110

VĀNAPRASTHĀŚRAMA AS A VRATA [S. KALYANARAMAN] 117

Vrata 117
Vrata in relation to āśrama 118
Vānaprasthāśrama 118
Vrata in relation to dharma 119

VĀNAPRASTHA IN THE WESTERN CONTEXT [GREESH C. SHARMA] 121

Introduction 121
Four Ashramas in Hindu Dharma 122
Learning in Hindu tradition 122
Grihastha Ashrama 123
Vanaprastha 124
Western Thinking of Retirement 125
The Rat Race 125
Concept of Freedom 126
Hindus in the West 128
Vanaprastha in the Western Context 130
Prescriptins and proscriptions in Vanaprastha 132

REPORT ON VĀNAPRASTHA VARGA, BLOOMINGTON, IL CAMP JULY 24-31, 2005 136

Introduction 137
The ideal Hindu American elderly 137
Creating vānprastha activists in the USA 138
Ethico-religious activism 138
Socio-cultural activism 138

Political activism 139
Economic activism 139
Legal activism 139
Healthcare advocacy 140
Academic and media advocacy 140
Appeal to Hindu Americans 141

APPENDIX I 142

Priority items suggested for discussion at Vānaprastha Varga: Bloomington, IL 2005 142

APPENDIX II 144

The ideal Hindu American elderly 144
Bibliography 145
Original Works in Sanskrit 145
Secondary Works 149
Abbreviations 157
About contributors 158

This book is dedicated in the memory

Of

Shri. Madhavrao Sadashivrao Golwalkar

Birth Centenary : 2006

Introduction [Shrinivas Tilak]

What is the perception of old age and aging Indo-American families have when they meet periodically to celebrate important family reunions or community events? When more than three thousand people attended the annual conference of the National Council on the Aging and the American Society on Aging in March 2006 in Anaheim, California, they were given a hand mirror: What image did they see in the glass when they held it up to their face? What is the image/s of aging they see in others? Is old age a dark period of decline, gradual loss of social status, and a source of ridicule? Or is it an uncharted territory of growth and opportunity? With this simple but effective exercize, conference organizers hoped to break down the wall between old people and the men and women who work on their behalf (Trafford 2006).

Organizers of the weeklong varga on the vānaprastha ideal in July 2005 "Meanings of old age and aging" in Bloomington, IL had a similar purpose in mind. The initial session explored the image problem the aged have among Indo-American families and how to train those who would like to act as facilitators of dialogue between the NRI community, its leaders, and the eldelrly. A comment that was often heard from the audience was that perception of old age and aging in the Indian tradition is positive whereas old age in the Western civilization is valued negatively. There is some truth in these comments. Laura Carstensen, chairperson of the Stanford University psychology department and director of its center on longevity and life span development, has similarly observed, "people in the field of aging are studying decline.""They are studying people who have problems."

Such a focus, however, can distort what it means to grow old. When Carstensen told a colleague about a study showing that people at older ages do better emotiuonally than youths or people in the middle age bracket, the colleague responded,"This just doesn't sound right." This response should not come as a surprise. She treats patients with depression. The challenge for many in the field of aging is to overcome this narrow, negative, medicalized view of the process of aging. "The narrative that has created this view is the narrative of decline. The narrative says that to understand aging is to understand decline," said Bill Thomas, founder of the Eden Alternative, an outfit that seeks to improve the environment of nursing homes. In today's North American culture a person in decline has no status (cited in Trafford 2006).

Another purpose of the week-long seminar on the vānaprastha ideal in Bloomington, IL was to present meanings of old age in the tradition of India and to render them relevant to the lifestyle of Indo-Americans living in today's America. Dr Shrinivas Tilak (he holds a doctorate in history of religions from McGill University, Montreal and is author of *Religion and Aging in the Indian Tradition* addressed the participants of the seminar tracing the evolution of the concept of *āśrama* (stage of life) as it comes across in the Veda, the depiction of old age in Sanskrit literary texts, and the meanings of old age in various moral and medical texts. Subsequently, he prepared articles on this topic some of which are included in this collection. Two other scholars (they did not attend the seminar but who are interested in the topic of old age and aging, Dr Srinivas Kalyanraman and Dr Greesh Sharma) were invited to contribute articles for this collection.

Gerontophilia, gerontophobia, and gerontocracy in the tradition of India

Vedic view of old age (gerontophilia)

Vedic culture reveals a distinct this-worldly emphasis on material prosperity, longevity, and progeny.[1] Since it is life affirming and life confirming, one comes across in them a distinct affinity with and appreciation of old age (gerontophilia). An Atharvan hymn to Agni pleads: Let not the treasure of old age be reduced; let it increase. Let Agni grant us long life of one hundred years (7:53.5-6). Another hymn to Sūrya opens with a request: May we see (*paśyema*) one hundred autumns (Atharva 19:67). The pleading for long life continues in subsequent lines with a different verb. May we--wake up to (*budhyema*); grow (*pūṣema*); adorn (*bhūṣema*); live (*jīvema*); prosper (*rohema*); be (*bhavema*). Another poet prays to old age deified as Jariman. Unto you alone, you Jariman, may this child grow. Let Dyau (sky) and Pṛthvī (earth) as the father and mother make you reach old age. However, it would appear that the Vedic life span was not marked by age specific phases or stages like childhood, adulthood, and old age. The metaphysical question of "why" of aging is not entertained.

---

[1] This account is based on Dr Tilak's opening address at the Bloomington, IL camp.

Buddhist critique of old age (gerontophobia)

The Buddha was dissatisfied with the Vedic life style where the 'facts' of birth, growth, and end of life are non-chalantly accepted as 'given.' He led a systematic campaign against this view of life which was to become the very raison-d-être of the Buddha's life and mission as a preacher. The uncertain and accidental life, he argued, justifies the passionate urgency with which the quest for spiritual liberation must be carried out in one's youth itself. Humans cannot afford to wait until they grow old, he declared. In the Buddha's teaching and message there is a profound aversion of aging and old age (gerontophobia) and its consequences (as the Buddha perceived them) illness and death. Nirvāṇa means securing one's escape from this triple source of suffering by following the eight-fold noble path.

The section on old age (Jarāvagga) in the Dhammapada undertakes a cogent and organized exposition of the typical Buddhist perception of aging as a biological process and old age as a cultural construct projected upon it. It discerns 'dependent co-origination' in the phenomenalization of the life process: from birth *(jāti)*, disease (vy*ādhi*), old age *(jarā)* to death *(maraṇa)*.

Compromise in the Dharmaśāstras (gerontocracy)

In the Dharmaśāstras (Manusmṛti, for instance) moral lawgivers like Manu sought to steer a middle path between the two diverging perspectives on old and aging that are discernible in the Veda and the Buddhist texts (gerontophilia and gerontophobia respectively). Manu attempts to reconcile the somewhat static Vedic desire for seemingly endless life with common, everyday dynamic human experience of finite span of life fraught with illness and old age that inevitably ends in death. Manu and other writers of the Dharmaśāstra like Yājñavlkya invested human life with definite meaning using a pattern of symbolism that would be commonly understood by the masses. Though the latter half of life is characterized by declining physical activities, Manu theorized that it is also a period of redefining the aging individual's status in his society as well as initiating the quest for self realization.

Accordingly, he normatively ordered human life in four overlapping stages of twenty-five years duration each. The stages are conceptualized as following one another in a constant and continuous process of cognitive and spiritual growth and fulfillment. They are traditionally identified as (1) the young student (upto age twenty-five; brahmacārin), (2) adult householder (from 25-50 years; gṛhastha), (3) aging hermit (from 50-75 years; vānaprastha), and (4) elderly wanderer (age 75 upwards; sanyāsin).

While the main task of the first two stages is development of outward-directed skills of mastering the ego; the final two stages are characterized by the quest for 'inner' spiritual growth and eventual self-realization. The process of aging brings about increased awareness and comprehension of new psycho-spiritual dimensions and emergent symbolic life, which was inhibited previously by the preoccupation with the external world. The stages of life theory are predicated upon belief that people are capable of increasing degrees or levels of knowledge, as they grow old. This is in agreement with Plato's view that we should undertake the study of philosophy (by which he means the long struggle to overcome the illusions of life) only after we have reached the age of fifty. Schopenhauer, in turn, also noted that as we age we develop through successive 'stages of life,' which give an increasingly accurate understanding of life's meaning.

The hermit stage is characterized as the ideal time for practicing a variety of austerities (*tapas*) to facilitate such developments. This prescription the aging hermit shares with the young student who is instructed to spend long periods of time in proximity to the fire tending it with fuel and reciting *mantras* in its presence so that the heat of the fire is absorbed and accumulated within the student. The hermit too is invited to 'dry up his frame by the practice of *tapas*.' If he can, he is encouraged to practice a severe form of *tapas* by standing in the midst of the five fires: four fires lighted in the four quarters with the blazing sun overhead. Thus the model of the student stage served as a prototype to integrate the values and practices of the competing heterodox ascetic orders who practised renunciation. Their practices were assimilated into the Vedic scheme of life by creating two additional stages of life: hermit and the renouncing wanderer. The hermit is literally one who stays or lives in the forest (*vānaprastha*). The *brahmacārin* similarly spent as many as twelve years as a student in one of the 'forest academies' that were usually operated and managed by the hermits.

Both the student and the hermit were required to keep the hair and beard and follow a strict regimen concerning food, sex, and sleeping pattern. Both kept the daily recitation of the Veda (*svādhyāya*). The norms and roles of the student, which clearly met the approval of the orthodoxy, thus helped prepare for the integration of ascetic's career into the Vedic fold as the hermit stage of life. The stages of the student and the hermit were clearly homologous with the former serving as a form of rehearsal for the latter.

This creation of the four-fold order is endorsed in an episode in the Mahābhārata where Sage Bhṛgu instructs Bhāradvāja that in days of yore Brahmā himself ordained the four modes of life for the benefit of the world and for promoting righteousness (Śānti 184:8-11). He then describes the duties, roles, and norms that each person occupying a given mode or stage of life ought to perform. Those of the hermit include cultivation of patience and fortitude. He should practice austerities near sacred waters and secluded woods abounding with deer. He should subsist on wild berries and roots. He should spend the day performing various sacrifices and sleep on the ground in the night bearing without regard cold and heat; rain or wind (Śānti 185:1-6).

The *āśrama* program is designed as a functional division where each stage of life is associated with a specific task: preparation, production, service, and retirement respectively. The four *āśramas* are to be lived sequentially and in chronological order. They interlock a rhythm of inner and outer direction. The student is inner-directed and his/her task is to prepare for life ahead. The householder and the hermit are both outer directed. While the householder supports the entire society including all those who are passing through the other three stages of life; the hermit shares his/her life experiences for the good of all. The wanderer stage is inner directed since he retires only after having contributed meaningfully to the community.

The Dharmaśāstras visualize an ideal organization of human life span into age specific duties, norms, roles, and values. It is predicated upon increasing association of function with age and the formation of segregated, age-based peer groups. They posit a direct functional link between age and a particular sphere of activity. The stages of the student and the wanderer are connected to acquisition of liberating knowledge (*jñānasambandha*). The householder and the hermit are connected to specific productiove tasks (*karmasambandha*).

A specific relation obtains between a particular *āśrama* and a specific *samskāra* (age-specific sacrament symbolically defined with reference to the type of sacred fire used in performing it). The stage of the student is confirmed by the tying of the sacred thread. The stage of the householder is confirmed by the tying together of the couple. That of the hermit is confirmed with the tying of the bark garment around the waist. In the case of the wanderer, however, the *samskāra* involves his untying from all social relationships and responsibilities. Upon formal initiation into the stage of the hermit, the vānaprastha proclaims, "I will tread the path of justice and righteousness; I will actively strive for the welfare my own self (*ātmakalyāṇa*) and welfare of the people (*janakalyāṇa*). I will scrupulously engage in the performance of sacrifice (*yajña*) and I will zealously engage in the cause of the spread of the Āryadharma."

The hermit's is an ideal stage for practicing of specific austerities. The Indian tradition believes that aging brings with it increased awareness and comprehension of new psycho-spiritual dimensions along with an emergent symbolic life style, which was inhibited in the first half of life under the spell of natural constitution (*prakṛti*). This insight compares with the thought of the German philosopher Arthur Schopenhauer who argued that as we grow older an increasingly accurate knowledge of life and reality unfolds. He compares the progress of life with the stitching of the garments we wear. The first half of life is like looking at the garment from the outside. One is charmed by its beauty, colour scheme, cut, style etc. However, in the second half of life one's attention is inevitably drawn inside. One then looks at the same garment from the inside. One then notices how it is stitched and how it is held together; where is is showing signs of wear and tear and the joints where it is likely to come apart if it is not maintained properly.

Old age and the elderly: a perspective from gerontology

The modern discipline of gerontology studies the science of aging, which is a biological process, and old age which is deemed to be a cultural construct. The Greek term for old age *geronton* is cognate with the Sanskrit *jaranta* (aging; derived from the verbal root *jṛ*). One perspective in social gerontology views aging as an inevitable withdrawing process resulting in decreased interaction between the aging person and others in the social system he/she belongs to. The process of disengagement is initiated by the individual or by others in the situation. His/her withdrawal is accompanied from the outset by an increased preoccupation with himself. When the aging process is complete the equilibrium, which existed in middle life between the individual and his society, has given way to a new equilibrium characterized by a greater distance and an altered type of relationship. The disengagement process focuses on the individual role-complex and the changes that take place in it as the person ages. Disengagement takes place earlier for some than for others due to differences in physiology, temperament, personality traits and life situation. Furthermore, the precise number of bonds broken with the society also depends on the individual's make-up.

As against this view of aging the activist perspective insist that continued and full scale activity (not disengagement) is the proper path leading toward adjustment, high morale, and life satisfaction in one's later years. The activity theory, however, fails to account for significant numbers of old people who do not cope satisfactorily in their later years. This has led some to question that a diṣti nction be made between an individual's role and his role set. Performance of any role (whether instructor, father or a worker) implies a reciprocal relationship between the performing actor and his social milieu. Execution of a role thus rests on the interaction between two or more persons, which then becomes the nucleus of other social relationships and systems.

Disengagement of the elderly therefore cannot imply a total withdrawal from all social relations but rather acquisition of a new set of roles. Disengagement occurs at different rates and in different amounts for the various roles in an aging individual's role set. Manu's ideal scheme for the hermit reveals a relative measure of concurrence between behaviour it recommends for the hermit and the concept of differential disengagement of modern social gerontology. The theory of differential pattern of aging would find support in Plato (*Republic* VII), which, as the Dharmaśāstras would have it, represents a middle ground between the activist and the disengagement theories.

The Dharmaśāstras calibrate the ideal organization of life span into age-specific duties, norms, and roles. They provide for increasing association of function with age and the formation of segregated, age-based peer groups. The *āśrama* program, as discussed earlier, is a functional division of life into four stages of twenty-five years each.

The four *āśramas* follow one after another in chronological order where emphasis unfolds from preparation to production, service, and retirement in that sequence. The four stages interlock a rhythm of inner and outer direction and orientation. The student stage, for instance, is inner-directed his task being to prepare for life ahead by acquiring proper education and learning a specific trade (*jñānasambandha*). The householder and the hermit stages are both outer-directed (*karmasambandha*). While the householder supports and sustains members belonging to the three stages, the hermit shares his/her life experiences for the good of all. The stage of the wanderer, again, is inner-directed. He/she retires only after having contributed meaningfully to the society.

The stages of life model is intended for the Āryas (i.e. those possessing a noble character.). It is important to remember that Ārya is not a racial term; it does not indicate membership in this or that particular race or caste. The Yogavāsiṣṭha defines Ārya as anyone who diligently performs assigned duties and desirable deeds and desists from doing deeds that should not be done.[2] It insists that noble character (*āryatā*) can be cultivated by any individual who practices yoga whereby even in the most ignorant individual arises the desire for attaining spiritual liberation.[3] The stages of life model skillfully harmonize the rights and duties of each individual (*vyaktidharma*) with his/her responsibilities to family and community (*kuṭumbasamsthā*).

Movement from one stage to the next is symbolically confirmed with reference to a specific sacrament (*samskāra*) and the performance of a prescribed ritual. The student stage, for instance, is confirmed with the tying of the body with the sacred thread (*yajñopavita*). The householder stage is confirmed by ritually tying the husband with his wife; the hermit stage by tying the body with bark garments (*valkala*), and the wanderer stage by untying the body and self from all bonds. The movement of the aging individual from the stage of the householder to the hermit for instance assures a smooth transfer of power and responsibilities in the areas of politics, military, administration, the corporate world, bureaucracy etc.

In the Indian tradition there are inspiring examples of Dhṛtarāṣṭra and Cāṇakya who were ideal hermits. By performing age-specific fire sacrifices and ascetic practices (*tapaścaryā*) Dhṛtarāṣṭra demonstrates how to use the natural biological process of aging for creative spiritual purposes. In the process he also teaches how to harmonize the *daiva* (the process of

---

[2] *Kartavyam ācaran kāmam akartavyam anācaran; tiṣṭhati prakṛtācāri yah sa ārya iti smṛtah (# 6: 54)*

[3] *Udeti yogayuktānām atra kevalam āryatā; yā dṣṛṭvā mūdhabuddhinām abhyudeti mumukṣatā* (# 6: 55)

aging over which humans do not have control, for instance) with *puruṣakāra* (old age, which is a cultural construct; see Dr Tilak's article on Dhṛtarāṣṭra in this collection). Cāṇakya voluntarily handed over prime-ministership of Magadha to Amātya Rākṣasa before he became a vānaprastha. He gave India and the world the magnificient treatise on public administration and political economics (Arthaśāstra). The hermit stage thus releases the individual to undertake self fulfillment on two levels: (1) preparing self for release (*mokṣa)* to be attained in the next stage of life (*sanyāsa)* through meditation and ascetic practices and (2) work for welfare of the community of which the aging person is a part (*ātmano mokṣārtham janahitāya ca).*

Dr Tilak's analysis of Aśvaghoṣa's two major epics (Buddhacarita and Saundarananda) suggests that the *āśrama* model facilitates the aging individual's need to substitute more easily attainable interests, activities and relationships in place of those they can no longer pursue successfully. It thus provides alternative sources of need satisfaction. Willingness and the ability to identify and engage in new and feasible pursuits come naturally with age. The culture and personality approach, which is implicit in the *āśrama* model, does not focus exclusively on the intra-psychic processes of the aging individual, nor does it deal entirely with the extra-social world of social relationships, institutions, and statuses. It rather addresses the articulation between the aging individual and his/her cultural matrix in terms of the constraints and restraints that he/she senses as limiting his/her behaviour.

Literature (as well as visual art) helps substantiate contemporary social conditions and cultural norms and events. As the human urge to create and improve, art is at the foremost in recording change. Pictorial art, sculpture and architecture provide a record for future generations to interpret and record aspects of human activities that now have become history.

Classical literature in Sanskrit is a veritable mirror presenting a faithful picture of the historical institutions as they existed in their last lap before disappearing in the changing sands of time in medieval India. This period is of great importance in the history of India as it was characetrized by three great empires: that of Harṣavardhana in the north, that of the Cālukya in the Deccan and that of the Pallava in the South. The literary output combined with surviving monuments of arts and inscriptions place in the hands of the students a mass of source material to reconstruct a picture of contemporaneous civilization styled as the golden age. While

Aśvaghoṣa and Kālidāsa lived in the beginning of the Golden Age of Indian history, Bāṇa and Kṣemendra came at the end of it. Classical art is a worthy supplement to our study of the texts. Both art and literature served like two wheels of a single chariot and soaked in the cultural amterial and milieu of their times. They help explain each other.

Dr Tilak examines Sanskrit writings from the classical period in which predominant concepts of old age are described. Sanskrit dramatic litearture offers countless instances, illustrations and characterizations for a common belief in old people's superior mental abilities. Great wisdom and mature judgment, for instance, are considered the natural heritage of old age enabling the old to be valuable advisors to the young. There is a literary tradition starting from Aśvaghoṣa and Kālidāsa and continuing through the centuries to Kṣemendra in which the ideal is perpetuated that old age is a crowning stage in man's life.

Tracing his family tree Bāṇa notes that Vatsa was the progenitor of Vātsyāyana clan to which he belonged. The Vātsyāyana Brāhmaṇas were householders but pursued the ideal of ascetics and therefore, were known as Gṛhamunis. This was a new epithet coined in the Gupta culture to identify saintly householders bearing the title of Vaikhānasa, who belonged to an important school of the Bhāgavatas. Among the mendicants who came to console Harṣa after his father's death were the Vaikhānasa monks. They were liberal and tolerant of women vānaprasthas. It may be that Kaṇva [father of Śakuntalā] was a Vaikhānasa. Lives of Vasiṣṭha and Janaka were their models. Pāṇḍuribhikṣus (who wore white clothes) also came to console Harṣa. They were rich mendicants who lived in luxury and kept elephants (cf Jātaka, Therigāthā) (Agrawala 1963: 136).

It is likely that the model of Gṛhamuni was initially devised to counteract the influence of the Buddhist insistence of discarding whole life in favour of monkhood. The Bhāgavatas, Vaikhānasas, the Pāncarātras, and the Sātvatas stuck to the householder's life while still taking on the moral and spiritual ideals of asceticism (Agrawala 1963: 30). Gṛhamunis eschewed communal dining (*vivarjita janapanktayah*) and cooked their own food. They were also known as Vidyādharas i.e. possessors of different lore and masters of various arts. Endowed with sharp intellect, they were unfailing in the performance of sacrifices. In Kādambarī, Bāṇa calls them *bhavanatāpasa* (Agrawala 1963: 31, 12). The vānaprastha was allowed to go to a forest with his wife; hence to an extent he was a *gṛhi*. But he had to conform to other rules which disti- nguished him from a *gṛhastha* (Yājñavalkya Smṛti 3:45-46.55). In the Rāmāyaṇa, Rāma seems to have fused the stages of the householder and the hermit while in exile and lived on fruits, roots etc. He was therefore a vānaprastha; as he enjoyed the pleasures of married life also, he was a householder. This shows the possible simultaneous character of the two stages of life.

Bāṇa describes Simhanāda, the general of Harṣa's army, who was tall like a Śāla tree. Though advanced in years, old age had not much effect on him. His eyes were veiled by brows whose wrinkled skin hung loose. His terrible visage was brightened by a thick, white moustache which hid his cheeks. The white long beard looked like a hanging fly-whisk (Agrawala 1963: 153).

Bāṇa describes preparations being made to celebrate the marriage of Rājyaśrī. Old matrons busied themselves in tying the knots on the clothes for the sake of their being suitably dyed (*purāṇapaurapurandhribadhyamānaih baddhaiśca*). Other old women finished the designs. Kātyāyanikā, an old woman having the experience of the ways of the world, was a personal attendant of Harṣa's mother, queen Yaśovatī (Agrawala 1963: 98-99,123).

Successful aging requires not only internal accommodation to one's own system of needs but also reasonable conformity to the demands of one's community. Like the Faustian ancient Indian aspired to have the full experience of the most diverse possibilities of human life. The Buddha saw in this thirst the basic cause of suffering. But Hindus did not dismiss this basic human instinct so easily. They sought to sample every aspect of human experience (albeit with restraint imposed by dharma and limited to a particular stage of life), which allows humans to exhaust them by plumbing their depths fully.

In a collection of this type variation in the writing style adopted by different writers is inevitable. Editors therefore have chosen to retain the particular style chosen by each contributor. Repetitions of certain themes in the contributions are also bound to be present. The discriminating reader is unlikely to miss them (particularly with reference to the discussion about the vānaprastha and the *āśrama* model). Hopefully, readers (both young and old) will also find here something that will offer more meaningful ways of relating to the biological process of aging and the cultural phenomenon of old age.

Chapter 1

Age sensitive grading of life span in the āśrama model [Shrinivas Tilak]

Introduction

In what follows below I seek to (1) discuss how disengaging action (*nivṛttikarma*) as the function of the realization that one is getting old is the principal motif and goal of the second half of life as it is conceptualized in the ideal stages of life model (*varnāśramadharma*), and (2) to broaden the semiotic and hermeneutic context in which to understand activities relevant to elderly healthcare and its promotion as a socio-cultural and ethical phenomenon. I thereby hope to contribute to a better articulation of the component parts of the discipline of comparative geriatric ethics.

Until recently few modern scholars besides Jung (1939) and Erikson (1950) had explored the potentials disclosed in the process of aging and in the phenomenon of growing old. Numerous experimental studies have reported decline--from failing memory to increased rigidity. Other studies have described what frequently happens in aging, rather than what optimally can occur. Such outlooks obviously miss the potentials of late-life development. Against this background, a general theory of aging and human development proposed by Chinen (1984), especially as it is applicable to late-life development, is a welcome change. The basic concepts of his theory derive from phenomenology and modal logic. Chinen hypothesizes that during development different modalities predominate at different stages and times of life. The general principle of logical modality asserts that the *mode* of a statement is independent of the *content*. There is a difference, for instance, between *what* a proposition says, and *how* it is said.

For example, we can say "Elders are wise" with (1) conviction and confidence; (2) merely raise it as a possibility; or (3) doubt its credulity in an expression, "Elders are wise?" *What* we consider (that elders are wise) is the same in both cases, but *how* we assert or qualify the proposition (the modality) differs drastically. Such a distinction between mode and content can be usefully employed, argues Chinen, to analyze experiences in the second half of life. In what follows below ' sentence (text), the four stages of life are the individual words (*pada*), which constitute it. The ideal of the stages of life model is 'work,' which can be interpreted in terms of the sequence of the four stages; and the roles and the norms of each stage of life.

Word and sentence are, both Prabhākara (the Mīmānsaka thinker) and Benveniste (contemporary French philologist and Sanskritist) argue, the two poles of the same semantic entity; it is in conjunction that they have sense and reference. The two are not mutually exclusive. But Paul Ricoeur (a contemporary French philosopher) posits a third pole (work) which he calls reference, in the understanding of a text. In this case 'work' refers to 'world' which is to be understood in an existential sense as a possible world for self-understanding and a potential mode of existing. It is in a word, a new way of understanding reality. The structure of the work is its sense and the world of the work is its reference. Hermeneutics is the theory that regulates the transition from structure of the work to world of work. To interpret a work (in the present context *varnāśramadharma*) is to display the world to which it refers by virtue of its arrangement (sequence of the four stages of life), its genre, and its style. The structure is to complex work what sense is to simple statement; while world of the work is to work what the denotation is to the statement.

Grading on the basis of age

The codification of life according to chronological age (i.e. age-grading) represents one of the most visible aspects of the standardized and bureaucratized life course in modern times. Since formal age criteria grant access to different social institutions (e.g. school, labour market, and retirement), the number and composition of institutional fields in which an individual participates may distinguish a life stage. Legal definitions related to chronological age seem to function as base-lines for various age typifications and age norms. For example, when an individual becomes legally eligible for Social Security benefits, he or she is soon thought of as 'old.' Analytically, we can distinguish age criteria for role assignment and status allocation according to their degree of institutionalization.

The life course as a social institution has been described as a system of rules that sort and categorizes individuals. Official categorization systems homogenize and formalize social meaning and social action. In the Indian context one important effect of the codification of social phenomena in the Dharmaśāstra is the reduction of the scope of possible meanings attributed to them, ultimately resulting in social consensus. The formal definition of age categories, for instance, involves the social construction of legitimate representations and legitimate practices granted to people of different ages. Age categories define the qualities, competencies, needs and motives (as well as rights and obligations) thought to be appropriate to the members of a given age group. They legitimize age-specific behavioral norms, which, in turn, structure the expectations of the members of the specific groups toward their own behaviour as well as toward the behaviour of the other age groups. In this respect, age status represents a set of socially defined and ascribed attributes, which, at the individual level, form the basis of a validated personal identity.

Life course: a cultural perspective

The culture's view of the life course and, especially, of life stages provides a general structure of meaning--an imagery, a language, or a set of symbols--within which people enact their lives. Individuals use these symbols and images to model their own life course and trajectories. This perspective may be employed to analyze the symbolic contents of specific life stages and to trace the changes these cultural patterns are undergoing. The discussion would then focus on the cultural imagery of adulthood and its current redefinitions. What kind of symbolic resources does the culture provide to shape the relationships between the individual and society in the public realm of life? As with the love image, action orientations in the public realm are not simply invented but are an integral part of a larger frame of organizing one's life. The work ideology (*artha*) offers biographical meaning to the individual's work life. In this respect it provides symbolic resources upon which individuals can draw to organize their own work lives.

Meaningful action

Meaningful action (such as is ideally envisaged in each of the four stages of life), like discourse, is subject to a kind of fixation and distanciation. There are, in fact, three characteristics of action which parallel the fundamental characteristics of the text giving rise to this possibility. Corresponding to the fixation of discourse in a text, while its event character disappears, is the fact that an action may be said to have the structure of both a locutionary and illocutionary act. The impetus for a model based on age-specific groups or cohorts can be understood from the work of the French psychologist Jean Piaget for whom aging is a source of community formation. Indiviudals share a network of age-related shocks that elicit common images of the world and common moral meanings. Piaget's contribution lies in the suggestion that people also share moral styles within age communities. Such age-informed communities function invisibly.

It would appear that the stages of life model renders the functions of such communities more implicit and visible. The prescribed roles and norms for each stage can be analyzed more meaningfully with reference to Norm Chomsky's (contemporary American linguistic philosopher) account of the derivation of a sentence. There is no simple left-to-right juxtaposition of structurally independent parts in a sentence. Rather, it is a top-down differentiation of wholes into their structurally dependent (and reciprocally implied) parts. The place occupied by an event in such a structurally dependent form may be defined topologically in terms of the superordinate event, which contains as a part. The model of life and its progression through different stages over the ideal period of one hundred years may be presented as follows:

childhood/youth	middle age/adulthood
old age	death

Topologically, today's event is the latest part of the structure to be derived so far, all other events can be found located or 'placed' between certain other events, and contained within more over-arching ones. Such a view allows the past to be revocable in the sense that different structures (as with Chomsky's ambiguous sentences) may be erected over the same flow of past experience. But the completed part of the structure offers to the uncompleted part only limited styles of completion. For example, tasks appropriate in youth are inappropriate in middle age. Living, therefore, has a grammar to it (Shotter 1980)

Age sensitive duties

The duties to be accomplished and a role to be fulfilled in each stage of life (*āśramadharma*) could be better understood if examined from the perspective of logical modalities suggested by Chinen and a logic of locutionary, illocutionary, and perlocutionary acts suggested by Ricoeur. Each stage of life has a 'propositional content' (a duty, role, and norm) which can be identified and reindentified as the same and which may, therefore, become an object of interpretation. Here a role is a patterned and stylized sequence of learned actions or deeds performed by a person in an interaction situation. A role represents the dynamic aspect of a status. As distinct from the individual who occupies it, status is a collection of duties and rights enjoyed by the individual. When one puts into practice the rights and duties, which constitute the statuses into effect, one is performing a role. To that extent, role connotes the structurally given demands (norms, expectations, taboos, responsibilities and the like) associated with a given social position. It is, so to say, one's inner definition of what someone in one's social position is supposed to think and do about it.

But one does more than just enact prescribed roles; one recreates or modifies them in order to make sense of the actions of others and to facilitate their own responses to them. When a person is 'merged' with a role in this manner, then attitudes and behaviour developed as an expression of one role are carried over into other situations or to another stage in future.[4] Norms demand that people do or be something or not do or be something. They also allow doing certain things, without necessarily requirng any specific thing. Age norms can demand that certain choices be made, that is, they can prescribe and proscribe specific behaviours or relations of the individuals to specific structural elements, but they also delineate a field of permitted behaviours and structural niches.

A given *āśrama* is comparable to an illocutionary act in that a typology of actions to be performed therein may be drawn up based on the constitutive rules designed for each *āśrama*.

---

[4]The manner in which individual and society are joined in a dialectical relationship in the *āśrama* model can be explained with reference to modern symbolic interactionism and phenomenological perspectives. Turner (1976: 1978), for instance, regards role theory as having an overly structured view of human behaviour and attempts to modify it by introducing an appreciation of the 'role taking' concept. He proposes the concept of 'role-person merger' as a way of understanding the degree to which the self becomes invested in the role. Many of the discrepancies between role prescription and role behaviour can be explained by the individual's inability to shed roles that are grounded in other settings and other stages of the life cycle (see Gadow 1986: 38).

Āśramadharma

The above two characteristics of *āśramadharma* give rise to what Ricoeur calls its 'sense content,' a sense content that is inscribed insofar as it leaves its mark on the overall temporal, individual, and social dimensions of the participating individual's life span. Corresponding to the perlocutionary act, third way the meaning of a text surpasses the event of discourse is the fact that a particular *āśramadharma* is an action the importance of which goes 'beyond' its relevance to the initial stage of life (*āśrama*). It may even be re-enacted in a later stage of life in a new context (norms of the student stage (*brahmacaryāśrama*) are to be replayed in the stage of hermit (*vānaprasthāśrama*), thereby establishing a new world of *reference* (in the manner Ricoeur uses it), which in a sense it bears within itself. Finally, like a text, *āśramadharma* a rational and meaningful action and an ideal type, is addressed to an indefinite audience. Like a text, which is open and accessible to anyone who is taught how to read, *āśramadharma*, too, is open to anyone who is willing to undertake a practical interpretation through ideal praxis.

Concluding remarks

If the correlation (as postulated above) between the *āśramadharma* and the paradigm of the text is valid, important hermeneutical and methodological consequences follow which are correlative with the place of explanation and understanding in text interpretation. Attempts to explain a specific action or (*dharma*) in terms of its motivational basis then must be similar to construing the meaning of a text. Such construal would begin with the preliminary understanding even if it be just a guess. And, just as explanation requires understanding; so too understanding is dependent upon explanation. And it must include a moment of appropriation as a climax of this process in reading. As a theoretical term the text serves to identify the object of hermeneutics and to delineate its task. Hermeneutics, in turn, is concerned with the interpretation of any expression of existence which can be preserved in a structure analogous to the structure of the text. The end result of this process of interpretation is self understanding mediated through appropriation. If now it is remembered that karma deals with a theory of rebirth based on the quality of previous lives determined morally, the six essential constituents for understanding the sequence of stages of life would be:

Six essential constituents

(1) Causality (moral or non-moral), involving one or more stages
(2) Morally responsible action: the belief that good and bad acts lead to certain predictable results in one or more stages
(3) Subjection of the individual to a cycle or round of roles and normative action patterns across stages
(4) Explanation and determination of duties and norms for present stage with reference to previous duties and norms, including (possibly) actions prior to birth
(5) Orientation of present stage of life and actions toward future stages, including (possibly) those occurring in new life after death
(6) Moral basis on which the performance in a given stage past and/or present is predicated.

Chapter 2

Caring for the aged in āyurveda: metaphysical, semiotic, and ethical considerations [Shrinivas Tilak]

The present study proceeds on the basis of the following hypotheses:[5] All medicine is practised in a paradox. On the one hand it offers seemingly infinite possibilities for sustaining and improving human existence. Debilitating diseases can be identified and organs can be transplanted. Each day genetic bio-engineering creates a new cloned species for the benefit of suffering humanity. Yet, on the other hand, the practice of medicine is constrained by limits. There is finitude to life since we will all die one day. There are limits to knowledge and to available resources. No other area of medicine highlights this paradox more clearly than geriatric and critical care medicine. Faced with this dilemma, we are forced to make critical moral choices and exercise options. Faced with the prospect and hope to do well we must decide how to act when we cannot do everything that is good.

Ethics of elderly healthcare

Ethics of elderly healthcare proceeds from a methodological focus on the experience of old age and begin with a central concern for the wellbeing of the elderly. Medical ethics can be expected to share in some important way this focus and this concern, if for no other reason than that aged constitute the majority of those who receive health care. Normative ethical judgments are usually made in the context of historical situations. If such a judgment is seen to have a broader significance than its practical application in a given situation, it becomes a norm and prescription. This process of application is based on the hermeneutical principle of analogy developed in the system of Mīmāmsā. Thus a new situation B may be considered similar enough to the old situation A to warrant the application of norm C in both situations. Norm C in situation B is based on its precedent in situation A. Only historical experience can enable this process of analogous application to be effective.

---

[5] Earlier version of this article was read at the annual conference of the Canadian Association for the Study of Religion in June 1988 in Windsor, Ontario, Canada.

Typical attitudes toward old age and aging

Typical attitudes toward old age and aging from the perspective of philosophy and sociology of geriatric caring action are couched in specific ethical maxims in the classical Indian medical tradition. Since medical ethics is shaped significantly by old age and aging, any discussion concerning it must be framed with reference to the reality of human aging and its consequences. The discussion that follows below is accordingly guided by the following set of questions:

(1) Is age a morally relevant characteristic? If so, are there significant moral requirements owed to old people because they are old?
(2) What is the rightful place of the elderly in society and culture? Do the aged infirm have a moral right to care and welfare if they did not produce anything themselves? What is the moral basis for asserting or denying claims of this kind?
(3) What is the human worth of the elderly? Do they have rights to care deriving from their former service to others and their long experience of life?
(4) The principles of caring and nursing ill and elderly persons to health in the Indian medical tradition are informed by cultural, social, and ethical constructs based on the doctrine of karma
(5) Indian medical tradition provides useful patterns for care giving, nursing and shaping health experience into a meaningful system of vital social values, ethical principles, and life goals
(6) Health and age-related statements in Indian medical texts are generally conceptualized in terms of social class, age, and gender (*varṇavayalinga*) .

In the classical Indian medical tradition such questions are discussed in an ambivalent manner. The general thrust is that age *per se* is only one of the three morally relevant characteristics; the other two being gender and class. Care is morally owed people for their productive potential and for service they may have rendered or continue to render to the state and the community. In the process interesting notions of health and disease emerge clarifying how their inputs factored into the proper range and scope of care giving in āyurveda.

Another important issue underlying ethical input in āyurveda is whether disease is an objective biological state explainable and verifiable by objective criteria alone or, alternatively, whether disease is also relative to social and cultural values. Āyurveda acknowledges that *both* disease and its treatment or prevention are conditioned by socio-cultural and religious factors. It therefore includes more penetrating reflections upon medical ethics than the casual reader might suspect. The principal concern is with identifying and collecting out of the scattered allusions in the āyurvedic literature ethical guidelines dealing with the role and duties of the physician with particular reference to the care of his aged patients. It initiates a discussion that might serve a basis for building a coherent hermeneutic and ethic that will serve as a bridge of discourse with medical practice in modern India and elsewhere.

On the basis of this data, ethical principles of contemporary relevance may be delineated were such arguments worked out. This is a somewhat unusual procedure for analysis of moral discourse, but it is dictated by the fact that no actual examples of extended arguments, either by physicians or by philosophers, are available in the Indian intellectual tradition. The principal source of reference for this purpose is the Carakasamhitā (Ca), the oldest surviving medical compilation attributed to Caraka, who is said to have been a physician at the court of King Kaniṣka (100 C.E.). Where warranted, reference is also made to two other relevant medical compilations--the Suśruta Samhitā of Suśruta (Su) (ca 400 C.E.) and the Aṣṭāngahṛdaya of Vāgbhaṭa (Ah) (ca 600 C.E.).

Healthcare in āyurveda

Contemporary interpretations of healthcare range from the narrow equation of healthcare with medical care to the broad inclusion of various activities that may have an impact on health although healthcare professionals not solely or necessarily perform them. One perspective, for instance, posits a sharp discontinuity between healths needs and other needs and desires. Health needs, thus, are held to be diṣti nctive and take priority.

Āyurveda, on the other hand, affirms continuity between health needs and other needs in that health is not viewed as an end in itself but rather, an opportunity to live life as formally prescribed in pursuit of the specific ends of life (*eṣaṇā*). With health energies can be directed to these goals. But when illness occurs, goal achievement is interrupted. Health thus is a complex concept connoting a homeostatic balance of the body for promotion of such ends as moral life (*dharma*), work, and material prosperity (*artha*), satisfaction of desires and family life (*kāma*) and spiritual liberation (*mokṣa*).

Health in āyurveda, therefore, is more than mere absence of illness; it is a positive force energizing one's existence, regardless of activity performance (*svāsthya*).[6] Such a perception of health is akin to World Health Organization's (1958) definition of health as a state of complete physical, mental, and social wellbeing and not merely the absence of disease or infirmity. Happiness and health, thus, are co-extensive terms. A secondary and gender-related definition of health is the ability to reproduce labour force. Women's activities as homemakers, wives, and mothers are crucial in the family's reproductive activities. Another important facet of health that is particularly emphasized in Indian medical practice is optimal ability to work and reproduce. The healthy person is one whose productive capacities extend in the areas of economics (*artha*), emotions and sexuality (*kama*), ritual and just behaviour (*dharma*) and spiritually (*mokṣa*).

The present discussion therefore focuses on the preventive dimensions of healthcare because in āyurveda the emphasis is on both the curative and caring forms of treatment for health. Āyurveda views the paradigmatic form of healthcare not critical medical care but rather preventive, long-term care which involves non-medical personnel and technology. Healthcare is considered as prevention of ill health and promotion of good health.

Nursing and caring action: metaphysical considerations

Health consideration at any age has both (1) theoretical and (2) normative dimensions. It is theoretical in that to understand health it is necessary to go beyond sense perception and reflect on what bodily constitution and functioning would be and should be. It is normative because understanding health provides a key necessary condition for attaining the goals of life; and from the overall Indian perspective, the last of the four ends in life (*mokṣa*). A philosophy may be understood as a system of

---

[6] Mhaskar (1954 2:12) refers to a related term for health *ārogya* which he explains as *ā* = till + *rogya* = potential of illness, that is, the state of the body till the person becomes liable to be sick. Health as *ārogya* is thus a balanced physical condition which may be thrown out of balance through negligence or other factors. According to Sharma (1985:12) *ārogya* denotes absence of disorder (*ārogya* = *rogābhāvād dhātusātmyam*). Indirectly, therefore, *ārogya* means balance of seven body constituents. But whereas *svāsthya* denotes the positive state of health, *ārogya* denotes the state of health in negative terms.

beliefs or values that influences individual or group action. It may or may not be articulated formally, but it is discernible through the proposed course of actions of individuals and groups. The metaphysics of gerontological healthcare focuses on beliefs about the nature of the older person. These beliefs affect many ideas regarding the relationship in a positive or negative manner. Metaphysics reflects on values held by those formulating the healthcare system which is then reflected in the caring and curing process. Developing metaphysics of gerontological healthcare would require analysis of the nature of life itself, the concept of aging, the concept of productivity, and the worth of the human being (Gress & Behr 1984: 194).

The metaphysics and philosophy of healthcare to which a given tradition subscribes influences both the selection of a model of elderly healthcare and the definition of health that guides healthcare. An elderly patient, who is treated with a lot of drugs and thus has a relative happiness in life, is still not necessarily a healthy person. Ancient Greek philosophy believed that medicine should deal with disease, rather than blemish of beauty or age. Not being beautiful (or young) is not sickness. In aiming at health medicine cannot and must not guarantee the pleasurable life. Similarly, the person who loses a limb [or who has grown old] is not an ill or sick person. One is simply not an able-bodied person one once was. Thus it proposed the able-bodied versus disabled (through age or disease) dichotomy, to be dişti nguished from the healthy versus sick dichotomy (see Plato *Republic* 405d). A somewhat similar stance is to be found in the āyurvedic metaphysics of healthcare.

Do older people have a right to exist simply because of they are human beings? How might the productivity of older persons, which includes nonmaterial as well as material productivity, be assessed in human terms? Consideration of these questions is crucial in geriatric ethics since concern is expressed by many over the use of healthcare resources by the elderly. In āyurveda, aging is viewed as a natural part of life and a disease. Both of these views affect the approach to medical intervention with respect to an older adult. In certain passages, the right of an older person to exist and to receive healthcare is questioned, especially if the person happens to be non-productive in terms of the traditional *varnāśramadharma* model.

In this context, an important metaphysical presupposition of Āyurveda is that positive health cannot be sustained by medicine alone. K. S. Mhaskar and N. S. Watve (scholars associated with the Board of Research in

Ayurveda, Mumbai) draw our attention to the argument that health must be sustained by appropriate goals and values in life (*artha*) and *karma* (appropriate motives, actions) in co-ordination with time (1954: 2: 4; *kālayoga*, AHS, su 12:19, 35, 57-59; Caraka su.1:20-23). Time determines the given stage in one's life and appropriate goals, values and actions for that particular stage in life. As a motivational concept sociologically, *goal* may be compared to the traditional Indian notion of *puruṣārtha*. A goal is understood as the outcome of a sequence of behaviours; it is something toward which behaviour is directed. A goal is a tangible outcome expected to result from satisfaction of a need.

Motivation, like other aspects of human development, changes with the passage of time. Developmentally, motivation has been conceptualized as occurring in four stages evenly spread over the life span. These phases are identified as (1) the growth phase (*brahmacaryāśrama*), (2) the engagement and creative phase (*gṛhasthāśrama*), (3) the disengagement and constriction phase (*vānaprasthāśrama*), and the transcending and liberation phase (*sanyāsāśrama*)(see also Buhler & Messarik 1968). Health may be lost on account of (1) impudence, (2) accidents, (3) biological limitations, and (4) ignorance. One is liable to commit faults leading to ill health in one's (1) daily duties toward one's self either through altogether neglecting, over-doing or under-doing them, (2) seasonal duties toward self by similarly neglecting, over-doing or under-doing them, (3) occasional duties toward self when subjected to undue influences of human or natural origin, and (4) conventional duties which devolve on the individual in each of the four stages of life (Mhaskar 2: 6).

Nursing and caring action: semiotic considerations

Methodologically speaking semiotics (the science of signs, *lakṣaṇāvṛtti*), is of central significance for understanding the nature of medical practice in the Indian tradition. Semiotic analysis of nursing and caring practices, therefore, is likely to provide significant clues for understanding issues relating to elderly healthcare in a cross-cultural perspective. Āyurveda may therefore be characterized a semiotic system in that it tends to gather at its disposal the necessary materials and techniques to produce, arrange, and interpret signs of disease and disorder which will yield socially and ritually appropriate and satisfying diagnoses and treatment. Consequently, āyurvedic texts make constant allusions to ideas of social and legal nature pertaining to health and healthcare, to be found in many influential *Smṛti* texts, particularly Dharmaśāstra. From a geriatric perspective the syntactic, semantic, and prognostic elements of old age events (see below) are also closely interwoven in āyurvedic texts and tell something of the history of life culture in classical India and much about the relationship between the elderly individuals and their social networks.

The diagnostic process in medicine involves tracing symptoms and signs to diseases. At times a patient may have many symptoms, but only some of them are important. The relation between symptom and the disease is an indexical one and the diagnostician must be able to trace symptoms and diseases that do not, at first glance, seem to be related. To do this, physician must have a profound understanding of the human body and how it functions. What complicates matters is the fact that a given disease may have a number of different symptoms or a given symptom may indicate a number of different ailments. It is the ambiguity of signs that makes them so problematical and makes diagnosis an art of interpretation.

Semiosis of old age

A semiotic perspective usefully offers a unifying framework that cuts across the boundaries of many academic domains. It also allows for the recognition of the analogies existing among the seemingly divergent fields of the social and medical sciences. Semiotics is a recognized tool in the analysis of the production, relation, and manipulation of signs which can be studied as they stand alone or as they come to refer within a specific context. Following Staiano (1986) it may be postulated that semiotics reveals certain general assumptions about culture, reality, and signs which are implicit in the general process of semiosis:

(1) Life processes, including aging, are ordered by signs. Humans structure and interpret their life experiences following pre-determined sets of signs
(2) Reciprocally, signs are ordered by life processes, that is, experience of the "real world" contributes to the creation and ordering of relevant signs
(3) No sign is ever completed, except through reference to another sign. This refers as well at the physiological or biological level.

Thus understood, what is the relevance of a semiotic framework to the analysis of healthcare in old age? It will be argued below that to explain old age means to describe how signs encoding the process of aging are linked to what they signify, how they are related to one another and the manner in which they are employed by the human beings in specific medical and socio-social contexts.[7]

Semiosis (i.e. the process of generating a figurative meaning by the production of appropriate signs) of old age takes place in three stages: syntactics, semantics, and prognosis. From a gerontological perspective syntactics describes the expression of aging signs, their order of appearance, and the assumed relationship existing among several such signs. The inclusion or exclusion of signs within a specific case varies according to the needs of the aging persons and the biological and cultural models which constrain them. In general the modern biomedical model of old age evaluates only biological signs produced by or about the aging body. The traditional āyurvedic model, on the other hand, also includes signs which are the product of social relationships, cultural values and ethical norms.

Since syntactics involves the relationship between signs, it must also deal with the ability of the signs to substitute or "stand in" for other signs. To use a simple example relevant to our discussion, one may determine by the mere colour of a persons's hair that he/she is elderly. The pulse or the heartbeat of the same person will lead the physician toward the same inference. Though the two sets of signs are not identical they can be substituted for one another for the purpose of drawing the inference that the person in question is elderly. Since this quality of 'standing for' another sign is related to the meaning aspect of signs, syntactics and semantics, though dişti nguishable from each other in theory, are not usually treated separately.

It will be argued below that for āyurveda; too, the relation of signs of aging to a symptom label 'old' is a semantic relation where semantics refers to that aspect of semiotics dealing with the meanings of signs before their use in a particular utterance. That is, such a label is assumed to have

---

[7] It is a tenet of semiotic studies that much of what we take to be natural is in fact cultural. Part of the critical enterprise of this discipline is a continual process of defamiliarization: the exposing of conventions, the discovering of codes that have become so ingrained we do not notice them. Nowhere is this process more important or more powerful than in our perceptions of our own bodies. Certain signs of old age as they function in language, in medical discourse, and in medical literature are the main objects of semiotics (Scholes 1982:127).

meaning or significance, which is intended to produce a precise response. The semantic dimension thus explores the relationship between individual signs and the explanatory models which are employed to make sense of a life process. But semantics deals with more than labelling or categorizing of signs. Through production, interpretation, and treatment of the signs of old age, for instance; seemingly disparate areas of life experience are connected and rendered meaningful.

Prognosis, the third phase of semiosis, examines the contexts in which signs of age occur and are interpreted and the manner in which they are exploited by individuals and institutions to some intended end. The signs that come to represent old age are polysemous, i.e., they "stand for" certain physiological and/or emotional states. At the same time they also serve to indicate or point to a past event, some supposedly causative fact. To that extent they imply an etiology. Signs of old age, then, can be are appraisive or evaluative. Since diagnosis is also a moral statement, a judgment about past actions of the individual and those who surround him/her, the evaluative aspect of signs [of old age] is of considerable socio-ethical interest and importance. Signs, in addition, point to the future. They imply or suggest certain expectations as to the future social status of the elderly as well as his/her future state of health and morale or lack of it. This is *prognosis*, the code which governs the expected course of events or sequencing of signs.

Because one of the objectives of āyurveda is to induce specific changes in an existing personal relationship or an alteration in social status of the aging individual; the utility of studying that objective in light of the semiotic framework outlined above in terms of syntactics, semantics, and prognosis should become evident. While the first two examine the production of signs by the body and by the social collectivity synchronically and diachronically; prognosis implies the ordering of future signs yet to be produced. Typically this involves an interaction between the aging individual and his/her physician, family or social group, and other professionals such as the nurse and the nursing aide who are responsible for carrying out the prescribed therapy.

We should at this point remember the context within which the āyurvedic doctor (*vaidya*) traditionally practised his art. Anatomy and physiology were quasi-inexistent, and the physician had no truly biological knowledge on which to base his actions. What pathology depended on, instead, was prognosis, the science of the course taken by illnesses and of the signs that herald accidents, crises, and solutions. Without the benefit of a developed knowledge of anatomy and physiology, the physician had no means of studying the affected parts of the body or the organic operation of the vital functions, in other words, he could make no local diagnosis of the disease. He was thus obliged to stake his reputation upon his prognostic skills. He was consequently less concerned to recognize the nature of a disease than to foresee the signs of its development, taking into consideration the most general conditions of life: climate, seasons, customs, postures (Zimmermann 1987: 20).

It was pointed out above how the application of semiotics in āyurvedic literature originates in the constant concern with the interpretation of signs of bodily dysfunction leading to old age and impending death (Carakasamhitā, 'Indriyasthāna' chapter one). The āyurvedic approach is semiotic in that it directs its inquiry into the nature of the changing relationship between (1) self and the aging body; (2) aging person and society; and (3) elderly patient and physician by producing specific signs for each. The signs of old age and disorders such as poor health related to it, whether objective (produced or observed by others) or subjective (offered by the aging), are regarded as non-arbitrary. The signs and symptoms which constitute old age require further interpretation in order to enhance, expand and transform them into information. This transformative process is determined by the various constraints imposed by a given medical and ethical theory: (1) the social, historical, political and personal contexts in which the signs are manifested; (2) the technologies available to the interpreter; (3) the variety of alternative interpretations available and; (4) the degree of accessibility to those interpretations.

As a semiotic act understanding old age involves the production of signs signifying the intrasubjective perception (initially at some unconscious level) of changed internal relationships which must come to be regarded, at this same physiological level, as potentially harmful to the organism. Physicians are sign producers, both in terms of generating signs signifying old age and those which signify ill or good health in old age. In addition to operating under a distinct ethical code to produce and evaluate signs of old age and health, the physcician is also social scientist who operates under a definite social code in supplying the interpretation. When signs are produced, either as symptoms or as intersubjective signs, they are made available for evaluation by self or others. This act is, in part, a communicative act that attempts to 'reorder' the disordered self. The sign in this sense, is a metonym for the self and an attempt to communicate the self in opposition to the other (I can describe the pain of old age to you, "the old person may be saying; but you cannot suffer and therefore cannot understand my pain.")

Old age, as a cultural event or experience, is inseparable from social, political, and economic realities. The image of health (ill or good, in youth or old age) is shaped by cultural practices and is managed from within cultural milieu. The experience called old age, its signs and symptoms as they are reported or expressed, the process whereby such signs are interpreted, are all semiotic phenomena. As such, they are subject to interpretation. It is not the mere presence of the sign/s of old age which is intriguing, but a hermeneutic, i.e. the interpretive process whereby these signs become information. In this context *interpretation* may be understood as the *process of transformation*, that is, a changing of form or structure. To the physician, for instance, information which may have been deemed 'meaningless' for others, gains 'significsance.' He/she transforms it in an idiom which allows for its 'clarification' and for its exploitation. Signs of old age may refer to definite dysfunction at the organismic level but they may also indicate far more. Being polysemous, they generate many interpretations, each linked to some cultural, social, or ethical domain.

Old age episodes, as narratives of personal health behaviour and of social and personal relationships, are hermeneutically instructive and significant. To the physician they provide models for and models of lived reality and life. Such episodes, occurring through time and across individuals become culture texts constituted of critical cultural elements (Winner & Winner 1977, Staiano 1979b). Episodes develop as personal and social myths displaying important information about the socio-cultural systems in which they occur and about the individuals who suffer them. They provide insight into the cultural realities, which constrain and motivate personal and group behaviour toward old age and health in old age.

Nursing and caring action: ethical considerations

Ethics of elderly healthcare proceeds from a methodological focus on the experience of old age and begin with a central concern for the wellbeing of the elderly. Medical ethics can be expected to share in some important way this focus and this concern, if for no other reason than that aged constitute the majority of those who receive health care. Normative ethical judgments are usually made in the context of historical situations. If such a judgment is seen to have a broader significance than its practical application in a given situation, it becomes a norm and prescription. This process of application is based on the hermeneutical principle of analogy developed in the system of Mīmāmsā . Thus a new situation B may be considered similar enough to the old situation A to warrant the application of norm C in both situations. Norm C in situation B is based on its precedent in situation A. Only historical experience can enable this process of analogous application to be effective.

Ethical analysis in medicine is concerned with exploring what reasons, if any, are given for specific choices and particularly the reasons that are moral in tone and character. The principal goal of this study is to broaden the context in which one may seek to understand healthcare and promotion as a socio-cultural and ethical phenomenon and thereby to contribute to a better articulation of the component parts of the discipline of comparative medical ethics. Toward that objective ethical principles in relation to elderly healthcare have been constructed by collecting, out of the scattered allusions in the āyurvedic literature to definite patterns of arguments which may be put together. On the basis of such arguments an attempt has been made to delineate, ethical principles of contemporary relevance, were such arguments worked out. This is a somewhat unusual procedure for analysis of moral discourse, but it is dictated by the fact that no actual examples of extended arguments, either by physicians or by social philosophers are available in the Indian intellectual tradition. The thrust of arguments turns out to be both teleological and utilitarian.

What reasons do āyurvedic texts give to justify elderly health care? Usually, two reasons are given (a) individuals desire to live as long as possible in a healthy, happy and active condition (*prāṇaiṣaṇā*) and (*dhanaiṣaṇā*), and (b) individuals, therefore, have a moral obligation to live as long as possible through the processes of rejuvenation and revitalization (*rasāyana* and *vājikaraṇa* respectively). But they give rise to specific ethical and practical difficulties when they are spelled out in terms of metaphysics of the physical body and social policy conditioned by it. In āyurveda the body (*śarīra*) is defined as that which is disintegrating and falling apart with every passing moment. The existential anxiety of falling apart is countered with care and attention (Desai 1989: 47). Āyurveda is also defined as the science of assuring a long and healthy life till ripe old age. The term is significant from both the gerontological and ethical perspectives. While *āyur* implies a long and healthy life span; *veda* refers to the science and technique of assuring it by submitting to a virtuous life style leading to spiritual liberation. The term āyurveda, by extension, designates a healthy, long life, which is a 'good' for which one should actively strive at every stage in one's life. It thus posits a clear diṣti nction between a healthy, happy life (*sukhāyu*) and a healthy, morally 'good' life (*hitāyu*). Health is a moral obligation incumbent upon every individual. Health, in fact, correlates virtue. Furthermore, positive, good health is a matter of moral duty and obligation, which is consciously and willingly chosen. It cannot be left to chance, fate or luck. Even ascetics are not exempt from the responsibility of maintaining good health.[8]

Health in āyurveda has one more important nuance; it implies ability diligently to execute assigned duties and tasks and reproduce as a responsible member of the family and community. The healthy person is one who produces prescribed ritual and moral merit (*dharma*), material goods (*artha*), emotional and sexual joys and satisfaction (*kama*), and spiritual liberation (*mokṣa*) in that order across a given life span. Health as ability to bear progeny destined for labour force impinges more particularly on women whose activities as wives and mothers are crucial in a community's reproductive agenda. Āyurveda, therefore, incorporates special sections dealing with thc health of women who are pregnant or nursing their infants. Activities which indirectly affect health status are known as *dharmakarma*, and as such, fall within the purview of the Dharmaśāstra. Direct health-related activities fall under the science of medicine proper (Vaidyakaśāstra). According to Suśruta, both the physician (*vaidya*) and the priest (*purohita*) are of equal importance in the preservation of health. The Dharmaśāstra texts, in turn, have chapters on physical and breathing exercises (*āsana*, *vyāyāma* and *prāṇāyama*). It is laid out that adherence to religious and ethical observances will promote good health. This is accepted by āyurveda, which holds that ill health results from actions originating in culpable insight or unrighteous behaviour (*prajñāparādha* or *adharma*.

Since medical enterprise is viewed more a means of preserving health than curing diseases, āyurveda lays much emphasis on dietetics as well as

---

[8] Ca.sū.1:15; see also Ah.sū.2:47). Aristotle's treatment of the role of physiology (and by implication of medicine) in the formation of virtue is also suggestive in this context. He held that the goal of medicine is not only health, but the improvement of individual moral conduct through the improvement of moral judgment.

on proper moral behaviour as means of insuring continued health even in old age. In fact, Caraka devotes four long chapters to these concerns in the section called "Sūtrasthāna." Elsewhere he traces ill health to unwholesome diet and improper moral behaviour, which is traced to culpable insight (*prajñaparādha*). This latter is believed to lead to various errors of judgment resulting in the derangement of the balance of the three humours (*doṣa*) and the subsequent manifestation of diseases. Disease is understood as a process of degeneration and inflammation, which is coeval with the passage of time and aging. If it is not treated in time a disease may lead to further deterioration and ultimately death of the sick individual. The wise and morally good persons, therefore, are those who avoid the intake of unwholesome food and thereby avoid premature ill health, old age, and death. The people for this reason hold them in high esteem.

In the āyurvedic doctrine concerning the regimen of health physical and psychological factors are blended in a peculiar manner in that they are sustained by a moral element (e.g. unhealthy desire is explained as uncontrolled desire). The ethical tone of āyurvedic texts ranges from the austerity of the medical student's initiation, leading to the pragmatic concerns for the reputation of the physician and his profession (Pellegrino 1979). As a moral enterprise Indian medicine duly refers to conceptual foundations and issues of professional ethics. It discusses such recurring moral problems in medical profession as deception, informed consent, privacy, collective responsibility, professional dissent, and justice. It also includes a standardized code of professional ethics.

Traditionally, Indian medical and moral digests explain (1) principles of healthcare, (2) what the penalties were for neglecting health, the degrees of their severity, and (3) the effective means of controls over resources and their use and distribution for assuring healthcare in terms of status, gender and age. Mixing nobility and practicality, these compilations reveal that concern for the patient is tempered by concern for enhancing the physician's practice and position in community. Āyurveda deems health to be virtue or at least an analogue of virtue. Health is also an indicator of virtue. Āyurvedic ethics, accordingly, appears to be teleological and utilitarian in orientation. A sick person develops a unique relationship to his/her disease, physician and society. Society and state thus reach into the patient/physician relationship: the state regulates prevention, therapy and rehabilitation; social groups govern various forms of support and immediate help. Thus both the physician and patient evolve a special network relationship to the state and society.

Āyurvedic texts include more reflections upon medical ethics than a casual reading might suspect. The relation of ethics to healthcare in āyurveda is at once pragmatic and utilitarian. The increasing rationalization of medical knowledge in the modern age, argues Naidu (1988), has led to a focus exclusively on disease, a bio-physical entity, rather than on illness, which is a complex social, psychological, and spiritual situation of the sick person.

Interaction between ethics and medicine

In light of the preceding the following six major areas of interaction between ethics and āyurvedic medicine may be identified:

(1) Ethical values shape and influence human mental and emotional states, which in turn, have a great influence on human health. Through conscious and subconscious myths, feelings and beliefs, these values are brought to bear on the ability of humans to enjoy good healthy life, to endure ill health and crises, and to cope with challenges and problems of old age and death.

(2) Medical science and ethical decision-making are rooted and nourished by such traditional Indian cultural virtues as charity (*dāna*) and compassion (*karuṇā*) in tending to the sick, infirm and the elderly.

(3) Explanatory models of health and disease of āyurveda draw on religious and cosmological presuppositions of pan-Indian culture outlined in the Sāmkhya and Vaiśeṣikā philosophies. The āyurvedic texts tacitly rely on these cultural arguments when answering such questions as "Why me," "Why did I grow old and become sick?"

(4) Both historically and at the present time people of Indian cultural background have believed that moral attitude and culture play a crucial role in therapy and curing.

(5) An important area of interaction between ethics, religion, and āyurvedic medicine comprises an extensive, though largely unresearched field, which Naidu (1988) designates 'health behaviour.' It is a large subdiscipline within the field of preventive medicine and includes a study of the patterns and habits that are associated with health, illness, and medicine.

These include habits of hygiene, diet, nutrition, and patterns of work, rest and recreation.

(6) Variables of age, gender, social class and occupation control health behaviour of a given community.

Various Śruti and Smṛti passages demonstrate how the Vedic, Śramaṇa, and Hindu streams in Indian tradition supported principles of healthcare and evolved the underlying ethical values. The various laws and customs are clearly constitutive of a definite system of values. Determining the various underlying assumptions can expose the cultural logic of this system. Mīmāmsā hermeneutical principles can be utilized for that purpose. The difficult ethical issues surrounding solutions to healthcare are conceptualized, legally structured, and treated as general guidelines or exceptions to them. The question what constitutes ill or good health in Indian tradition is explored through the data on the historical dialectic between the Brahmaṇa and Śramaṇa streams of thought and their accommodation in the composite Hindu medical stream as reflected in classical medical and moral digests. The objective here is to understand how the ethico-legal systems of Hinduism have structured the notions of personhood, health, illness, self-care, and responsibility for good health, the impact of social class, age and gender on these considerations.

Care and its delivery (*śuśruṣā*)

The act of caring incorporates various health techniques and related moral decisions which render it an ethical enterprise. Caring, in the typical Indian way of life, is the outcome of four intervening agents and their prescribed actions: the physician, patient, medicaments, and the nursing attendant.[9] Every decision pertaining to care (giving or receiving) involves the complex interplay of value sets of these four agents. The importance of ethics in Indian medicine, therefore, cannot be reduced to pious appeals to its practitioners, but rather, a necessary and productive basis for evaluating and delivering health care. In moral philosophy sentiments alone are not enough; mere evoking of compassionate sentiments does not inform us about the right thing to do in a given situation. Āyurvedic ethics, therefore, is grounded in certain key virtues, which are seen as habits and dispositions that may enable a person to reason well. To find appropriate and legitimate ethical principles and categories for

[9] Ca.sū .9:3.

developing a sound healthcare delivery, Caraka and other writers on Āyurveda turned to Dharmaśāstra texts, which prescribe age-, class-, and gender-specific injunctions designed to encourage a virtuous mode of life (*varnāśramadharma*).

Delivering health care

The process of delivering healthcare in āyurveda, therefore, reveals certain morally implied assumptions about the nature of (1) healthcare and its delivery, (2) the patient-physician relationship, and (3) the ideal and good healthy life. Healthcare and its delivery presume a somatic view of disease and health. To that extent the physician rules supreme since he is the one who "saves life."[10] Yet, the medical enterprise of health care is also posited in functional terms since disease is viewed as inability to function effectively and efficiently in society. The etiology of disease is traced to significant deviation from a prescribed ritual or social norm prescribed for that particular individual. This invests the sick (and, therefore the dysfunctional being) with typical social meaning of being deficient in a particular value. Health and illness, then, become not merely somatic conditions of individuals; they are also defined and institutionalized through their social nexus and structure. Whether one is formally designated healthy or ill has significant bearing on the performance of one's social tasks and standing. Medicine and health care delivery become a set of intersecting roles fulfilling a specialized function within an encompassing set of social roles. Though it is recognized to have roots in biological causes what gets labelled illness or old age is a function of social and ritual precepts originating in the doctrine of *karman.*

Ethical issues in relation to health care and its delivery, therefore, presuppose both a physical and social nexus and are discussed in terms of the ideal relations between the physician and his patient and family. What the physician is asked to do morally is to be based on his insight as a physician as well as his perception of the relevant social roles. His education and training is intended morally to qualify the future physician for his profession. More broadly, healthcare becomes a function of particular set of relationships established by a community to attend to the quality of life and to promote the well being of its members. Medical ethics then raises the question of where the primary focus of healthcare might

---

[10] Ca.sū .29:4.

be. Is it with the physician or with patient? Āyurveda seems to imply that *both* are equally implicated since *both* are moral agents.

The āyurvedic teaching which insists that everyone is morally responsible for promoting health through self care and effort has clear cross-cultural scope and application. In modern times, self care is emerging across the world as an innovative and challenging dynamic within the health care system generally and within geriatric ethics specifically. In the past the medical profession alone was deemed to be totally responsible for the health of the patients. This custom is now slowly giving way to a general consensus that the responsibility for health maintenance also resides with the individual. This reversal of trends resulting in the promotion of self care movement has elicited theories from many health professionals. Self-care is defined by one group of scholars as

> [A] process whereby a lay person can function effectively on his/her own behalf in health promotion and illness prevention and in disease detection and treatment at the level of primary health resource in the health care system.[11]

The self-care movement based on such lines attempts to incorporate both the personal health behaviour and the social skills of laypersons to aid in the acquisition of proper health care. It is based on the understanding that patients who are active rather than passive in maintaining their own health status, even in old age, through personal behaviour and health practice.

Ethical dilemma of the elderly patient

Āyurvedic texts view aging to be *kālaja,* that is, it is initiated and sustained by time (*kāla*) from the moment five basic elements (*bhūta*) and the self (*ātmā*) come together to produce life. Old age, as the epiphenomenon of the general life process (aging), manifests itself in the due course of time. As such, aging of the body is an unstoppable, irreversible and inevitable process. No therapy can arrest it or cure the diseases, disabilities, and discomforts engendered by it. Potentially, therefore, any geriatric therapy may only delay the onset of old age and/or help manage and cope with the stresses of aging. From an ethical perspective, the relevant issue is: (1) to

[11] Levin et al (1978, 17).

what extent is an individual responsible for his/her illness which may be traced to that individual's particular life style? and (2) to what extent the individual himself/herself or some other party should be made to accept the burden of illness or the costs of treating diseases associated with old age?

Caraka's answer presumably would be that there is no general moral entitlement to health care simply on the criterion of old age.[12]He, however, seems to recognize a claim to care in the event of 'premature aging,' which is viewed as 'disease.' The ultimate cause of premature aging is usually identified in karmic terms. The root cause with a person 'who ought not to age,' is the premature exhaustation of semen (*śukra*) or the relatively positive 'reproductive' karma that gave rise to the particular life and its span and quality (Tilak 1989). Labeling aging disease is one way of identifying a condition, which is deemed to be controllable and manageable (within certain limits) with the help of a proper preventive therapy such as *rasāyana*. Typical geriatric therapies of rejuvenation and revitalization therefore may be construed only as coping mechanisms of (1) delaying aging, (2) preventing premature aging or impotence and, (3) providing energy to be able to accomplish the prescribed tasks in old age provided the therapy is undertaken as a prophylactic measure in one's first stage of life (*brahmacarya*). Under certain extenuating circumstances man may undergo them while he is a married householder and without a son but in any event they must be completed before he leaves that stage. To speak of premature aging as a disease would also entail some notion of its being improper. The sense of impropriety, however, cannot be based on aging being unusual; since everybody grows old. Only 'premature aging,' under the circumstances, may be judged unusual when it occurs in an individual prior to its usual occurrence in most humans. The āyurvedic category of 'premature aging' thus appears interesting from a cross-cultural perspective because it advocates that elderly individuals need not be abandoned as useless but given proper treatment so that they may resume and maintain their roles as useful members of society.[13]

---

[12] For the sake of comparison, see Daniel Wickler (1987) where the theme is developed from the modern ethical standpoint.

[13] Compare with Talcott Parson's (1979) argument that labelling people sick puts them within the sick role and confers on them medical attention. Similarly, by labelling them sick, one might expect to ameliorate the condition of those who are prematurely aged.

Ethic is primarily concerned to explore what reasons, if any, are given for choices of specific actions, and particularly the reasons that are moral in tone and character. In the present context geriatric ethics would be concerned to explore why *vājikaraṇa* and *rasāyana* are 'right' or 'good' preventive measures to be applied in youth or middle age. In a discussion of the extension of active life, it is quite apparent that a valuation is already implied in the stipulation of these practices that these are intended for the purposes of enabling the individual in question to asure good health and vigor for the purpose of attaining liberation or progeny respectively. Such a rider or reservation seems to imply that there are reasons for not considering the prolongation of simply human biological life itself as a worthy purpose. The concepts of *mokṣa* or *puruṣārtha* suggest certain human capacities that are either of value in themselves, or are the conditions (and thus of instrumental value) for realizing or achieving other values.

Right to healthcare in āyurveda

Like other ancient languages such as Hebrew and Greek, Sanskrit, too, does not have equivalent expressions for the modern term "rights". Yet there is evident in āyurvedic texts a certain correlation between rights and obligations. What is Y to which X has a right and which Z has an obligation to provide? Medically, argues Childress, the content of such rights is identified as health, not healthcare. It makes no sense, however, to talk about a right to one's health as a negative right--a right not to have one's health damaged by others. If a right to health were conceived as a positive right, it would impose impossible demands upon the society. It is, therefore, not possible to guarantee or to ensure health--and any attempt to do so would exhaust the society's resources. Several classes of obligations do not entail rights. Duties of charity, love, and conscience, enjoined on the physician, often function as self-appointed services than moral requirements. Duty and obligations, therefore, may refer to any required action whether the requirement derives from a right, a matter of conscience, a supererogatory ideal, or some other source. As per āyurveda, healthcare is individual's duty and not a right. Unethical lifestyles and behaviour patterns correlate significantly with premature aging, old age and death. Does an individual have a right to healthcare if he/she has not fulfilled the duty of self-healthcare? The āyurveda answers in negative. The independence of the older individual is a major goal of geriatric ethics. Its theoretical framework revolves around the concept of self-care. For, it is in self-care that the ultimate independence, decision-making, is incorporated into one's life. The older person is judged as being capable of initiating self-care and self-help.

Success in self-care rests on the older person's resources. When self-care is initiated, the older person acquires a futuristic orientation to health goals. To give the elderly client hope and optimism is very important in promoting self-care. Self-belief is crucial for believing in others and helps to dispel older person's feelings of being a burden to society and to their families (Grace and Bahr 1984: 136). Āyurvedic ethics posits a meritarian standard for distributing finite resources for healthcare. (1) Healthcare needs, it claims, are deserved. Health in old age results in varying degrees from people's own choices and actions in their younger years, (2) Health and illness in old age are much more socially determined rather than individually determined, (3) Right to healthcare in old age is forfeited if a certain level of responsibility is not met. But it is difficult if not impossible to pinpoint responsibility.

In other passages provision of healthcare in old age is seen as a matter of beneficence. It therefore is not as strictly laid out an injunction. It is an important obligation, though not a perfect obligation involving correlative rights. In addition to the language of imperfect obligations, the loss of ideals can also establish important moral reasons for providing medical care. The language of virtue and character, which expresses another kind of "agent morality" also bears on the allocation of resources for and within healthcare. Although, on occasion, there are strongly enunciated imperatives to extend healthcare to the destitute and to treat the poor gratuitously, āyurveda nonetheless holds that the best way to improve healthcare is to focus on the preventive aspects of social and clinical healthcare. Better diet and body discipline, for instance, may improve healthcare more than treatment per se can.

As a dietetic medicine āyurveda is a method of preserving health by regulating one's regimen and dietetics (*āhāra*). Gadually, it evolved beyond mere restoration of health and became a means of insuring continued health by preventing disease. Dietetics soon incorporated the ethics of the body whereby preventive medicine became a counterpart of ethics. Healthy body and mind became a prerequisite of ethical duty (*dharma*). By assuring a healthy body, sane nutrition, and a sane lifestyle one also assures success in the goal of liberation (*mokşa*). There is awareness that merely knowing one's duties in the practice of medicine is not enough. The physician himself must also develop an appropriate moral character. Moral struggle in the fulfilment of duty emerges when the physician is tempted to act on his own self-interest rather than the interests of his patients. The virtues to be cultivated are listed in all the three major medical texts. Thus āyurveda may be called a goal, duty, and virtue based ethical theory and philosophy.

Ethics of healthcare is composed of an inner structure consisting of the physician, the patient, and the society/state. Its outer conditions comprise of social and cultural inputs to the healthcare process. Since the task for āyurvedic ethics is to find appropriate and legitimate principles and categories for dealing with its problems, the physicians turned to the law givers and their moral digests. For, by their very nature, the Dharmaśāstra literature is designed to deal with particular cases, rules, and concepts which are much easier to apply directly to concrete situations such as illness than are formal and abstract principles such as utility. One unanticipated consequence of this development has been that āyurvedic ethics became fraught with legalism, i.e. the ethical attitude that holds moral conduct to be a matter of rule following, that a moral relationship consists of duties and rights legitimated by Dharmaśāstras.

Scope for cross-cultural research

The foregoing attempt, it is hoped, would suggest avenues in which the medical profession in contemporary India can engage in a meaningful dialogue with its traditional counterpart. Health professionals and caregivers in contemporary India tend to restructure healthcare delivery closely along lines of an idealized model of professional care in technologically advanced west. They tend to treat healing as if it were a totally independent, timeless, and a culture-free process to be understood either as an isolated special case or by comparisons with western clinical practices, psychotherapy etc. They do not regard healing as a care function of healthcare systems to be studied in its own terms within specific social and cultural contexts. This borrowed policy and perspective does not correspond to the actual situation in the Indian world where a large majority of old age and illness episodes are treated in the family context of traditional healthcare systems. The self interests of the healthcare professionals militate against using more extensively the traditional healthcare system models such as the āyurveda, which are closely tied with cultural, religious, and ethical concepts and concerns. This has distorted and delayed informed evaluations of self-care and treatment by indegenous practitioners, along with research on how these traditional therapeutic approaches might be used in state planning for healthcare services (Kleinman 1980: 32).

Contrary to the trends in modern west, the healthcare model that āyurveda advocates calls for the analysis of healthcare systems in the same way that religion and kinship systems, language or other symbolic systems are analyzed. It is, therefore, necessary to study the relationships of a healthcare system to its context. Cultural settings provide much of the specific context that characterizes healthcare systems. It is the transactional world in which everyday life is enacted, in which social roles are defined and performed, and in which people belonging to different age groups negotiate with each other in established status relationships under a system of religious and cultural rules. Current interest in philosophical and ethical dimensions of modern medicine must be brought in relation to the past semiotic and ethical perceptions in the Indian tradition on descriptions and interpretations of what it means to be sick, of medicine as therapy and the relation between patient (elderly and non-elderly) and physician. The traditional Indian medical systems are open and receptive to such a dialogue. Asking following questions may delineate trends supporting ethical reflections on aging:

(1) Did ancient Indian communities value older people sufficiently to do what was needed?
(2) What elements that dominated Indian society then still continue in the present ambivalent attitudes toward both aging and old people which are fuelled by such factors as modernization, industrialization, nuclearization of family, and population mobility?

While in the past the Indian medical tradition restricted healthcare in favour of wealthy, middle aged males possessing a higher social status, future Indian generations may opt for a priority with regard to healthcare benefits in favour of the side of the elderly females (since they are likely to survive longer than elderly males). In between these two extremes present Indian nation must look anew for bridges between competing age groups and genders in such a primary arena as healthcare. It must also find ways to promote bonding between genders, generations and ethnic and linguistic groups. It is in this context that information recovered by the present research is likely to be useful.

Comparative ethics of healthcare

Comparative ethics of healthcare has become increasingly aware of the worldviews and patterns of moral values imbedded in the textual traditions of different cultures. The present study concerned itself with how the elderly healthcare is perceived in the classical literature of Indian medical tradition using a semiotic perspective. As explanatory constructs, this evidence needs to be interpreted in light of the current views of health promotion since the traditional Indian medical texts contain a sophisticated theoretical reappropriation of a varied set of textual and societal material, interpreted, and arranged deliberately and consciously. To be sure, materials considered above represent the views of a particular class of elites who, like intellectual or religious elites everywhere, construct views on health, which lie between the descriptive and the prescriptive. Such views, therefore, are not entitled to be considered the articulation of *the* meaning of elderly health and healthcare.

At critical transition periods, when values must be forged anew, there is a basic responsibility to be fully informed of the possible repercussions of modernizing trends on a traditional society. If these trends are contentious and subject to agitation by lobby groups, then there is even more reason to be vigilant in order to find out what the trends are and how these will affect individuals, minorities and society at large. Further research in the area of elderly healthcare, for instance, is warranted since there are serious ethical issues involved in the determination of effective principles of allocating scarce resources to healthcare of people in all age groups. One important kind of analysis of humanities involves studying the history of the phenomenon in question.

Since one of the basic concerns in most modern nation-states is to develop better means of allocating scarce resources to healthcare, we need to know as much as possible about what different solutions have been suggested and applied in world history. How has this question been understood in the past? How have social structures, especially the religious and ethical dimensions of healthcare, coloured the issues of equitable distribution of finite resources? How have different societies and cultures found ways of defining and maintaining good health and its corollaries- self-care and self-responsibility? What are the suggested ways of dealing with old age and accompanying ill health? To avoid problems of ethnocentrism and reductionism in a pluralistic and multicultural democratic nation such as India, we need to evolve a more comprehensive and broadbased framework and outlook.

Such an exercise, it is hoped, will help promote a wider scope and focus on ethical perspectives of elderly healthcare in Canada. Almost a quarter century ago in 1974 a federal publication entitled *A New Perspective on the Health of Canadians* put forward a view that people's health was influenced by broad range of factors: human biology, lifestyle, the organization of health care, and the social and physical environments in which people live. Yet, present demographic trends also suggest that costs of existing health care programs for Canadians will continue to escalate. Public perceptions of those who are elderly, dependent, and in need of care, could change as costs of programs increase. If the elderly, the poor and the sick come to be regarded more as a burden and problem, health care programs could come under critical scrutiny. Programs for the aging, in particular, are likely to encounter increased competition for limited funds in government budgets. Canada has performed fairly well in controlling the growth of health care costs; however, cost control is a matter of continuing concern. The pressures created by an aging population and the growing incidence of disability will take a heavy toll on financial resources.

So far, there is insufficient information upon which to make informed decisions about these issues. In the healthcare system pertaining to the elderly, for instance, the transfer in emphasis from acute intervention to management of the complex socio-medical problems of the aged is only beginning to take place; as is the shift from early placement in institutional care to imaginative hospice or home care. A more realistic and reasonable ethos about allocating scarce resources to the health care of the elderly has yet to emerge. As debate over the costs of health care emerges, it is important to know how these issues are addressed in other cultures and traditions. A comparative perspective may help inform the contemporary debate. It is in this context that much can be learned from further study of the ideals, values, and social networks concerning hermeneutical strategies of health promotion in the Indian medical literature, a civilization and a tradition with a long history of survival.

A methodology for embarking on such a study would involve textual exegesis and interpretation in order to elucidate the various stages in the evolution and characterization of medical ethics as it pertains to healthcare in Indian medical tradition. Location, translation, and interpretation of relevant passages from classical literature in Sanskrit with reference to the philosophy and ethics of health care and promotion must be carried out along a similar line of inquiry. The data then could be analyzed in light of contemporary theories of gerontology, semiotics, and hermeneutics in order to clarify and shed more light on the recent debate on issues of healthcare.

Chapter 3

Depictions of old age in Sanskrit literature [Shrinivas Tilak]

Introduction

It is generally acknowledged that the symbolic reality shaped as culture confers specific meaning and significance on various life processes, including aging. Relevant cultural ideas on aging are not only shared but also manipulated by persons and groups to resolve particular problems of meaning by mediation through linguistic signs (words). Such an expression and investment of meaning in terms of language is ubiquitous--from our definitions of the physical world and the social reality to our conceptions of other worldly realms and even the existential domain--so that, human pain and suffering are endowed with typically cultural meaning.[14]

In Indian tradition, the concept of *samvṛti*, first espoused in the Vedic literature and then suitably reinterpreted by the Buddhists (Samyutta Nikāya, 3:70-73 for instance) is roughly equivalent to the modern notion of symbolic reality. *Samvṛti* (the Pali equivalent is *sammuti*) literally means agreement, and by extension, conventions--linguistic, social, political, and moral. In the pre-Buddhist Vedic texts such conventions were elevated to the level of absolute realities permanent and eternal (Ṛg 10:125). But in reinterpreting *samvṛti*, the Buddha argued that these conventions are not to be clung to as absolute truths, nor to be dismissed as mere conventions (Kalupahana 1986: 17). In other words, language is neither the faculty of speech nor the goddess representing the ultimate reality (Vāc); nor is it unable to express reality (*vikalpa*). He rather argued that language derives its meaning only when it is able to communicate

[14] This view of the specific relation between language and meaning is endorsed by Benjamin Whorf's work on comparative languages (1965). Inuits, for instance, have a wide range of words to denote different kinds of snow, but only one word for many objects for which other languages have a number of words. Whorf has shown that these differences in language largely reflect the different ways in which people conceive reality. The particular syntactical and grammatical properties of a given language faithfully reflect the patterns of the symbolization of reality.

results (*artha*). Thus, that which bears result is alone true.[15] In a similar vein Bhartṛhari (ca.600 CE), the Hindu grammarian and philosopher, also asserted that word (*śabda*) forms the fundamental essence of all things (*artha*).

Thus understood, language is closely tied with meaning in all human activity. For instance, since humans cannot rest content with the mere fact that one inevitably grows old and dies, they must reflect on the phenomenon of aging and verbalize it to express specific meaning (*artha*) whether in positive or negative terms. In India it was realized very early that it was not very meaningful to posit that aging was merely an accident or a chance event as schools of Indian philosophy such as the Ājīvikas did. On the contrary, the personal as well as public experience of aging was immediately invested with specific meanings when the Purāṇas began to argue that aging was the consequence of (1) bad karma in this or past lives, (2) the movement of planets or (3) the drying up of vital energy (*vīrya*) attributable to different factors.

Semantic domain of age

Semantics is here understood as the study of meanings and how they are expressed and communicated. Meaning in its various modes has to be articulated in language and the peculiarities, richness, stylistic predilections, and limitations of a language both facilitate and set barriers to the ways in which meanings can be generated and understood. In Indian linguistics, words as labels for specific things are considered to be the basic units of meaning. Technically, such units are known as lexemes or lexical units (*pada*). Whether singular or disconnected, they are generally associated with other similar lexemes into diṣti nctly identified classes or categories (*vargas*) which, in turn, are organized into still larger groupings (*kāṇdas*). As a distinct and larger semantic domain, *varga* consists of a class of objects all of which share at least one feature of meaning differentiating it from other semantic domains. For Indian lexicographers age is an important semantic domain because (1) it is a universal feature of human life based on differential maturity and time, and (2) by being primary, age along with class and gender, is an important

[15] This claim is made in a discourse by the Buddha to the prince Abhaya who was coached and sent by Nataputta, the Jain, to trip or trick the Buddha in the debate (Abhayarajakumara Sutta, Majjhima Nikāya (1:387-392).

component of the statuses and role models in Indian tradition. The custom of using language as a register of class, gender and age has been well entrenched in India at least since classical times. A person's deference toward another is clearly demonstrated in explicit verbal acknowledgements of his/her own status in terms of lexemes suggestive of age, class, and gender.[16] Age in Indian tradition is a semantic domain with several lexical markers delineating various divisions within that domain (young, mature or old); in terms of genders. It serves as a gloss for age-specific norms, roles, statuses and expectations that Indian tradition uses to organize human progression through the life course.

One important Sanskrit lexicon, Amarakośa, attributed to Amarasinha (600 CE), for instance, is divided into three sections (*kāṇdas*). The second section of this work includes the topic entitled the semantic domain of 'man' (manuṣyavarga). Here we find listed eleven synonyms each for man and woman followed by lists of synonyms for terms designating various age-specific phases in the male and female life cycle. What do these age-related lexemes and expressions have to do with the process of aging, and what do they have to do with each other? It will be argued below that their categorization is not random. Rather, it suggests a deliberate and coherent conceptual organization underlying similar expressions.

Such organization of words denoting various phases in the human life cycle indicates that in Indian tradition age is an important semantic domain and a universal feature of the human life process based on differential maturity and time. This is clear from the fact that the Amarakośa (2:6.7ff) dissects both the male and the female life cycles into three main phases and labels each with clear and concise terms. Childhood (*bālyam*), youth (*tāruṇyam*), and old age (*vṛddhatvam, sthaviram, vārdhakyam*) constitute the phases in the male life cycle. The female life cycle begins with 'first age' (*prathamavayasi, kanyā, kumārī*, 2:5.1089), that is, 'without menarche' (*adṛṣṭarajaskāyā*) followed by the 'middle age' (*madhyamavayasi*, 2:5.1090), that is, 'having the first incidence of menarche' (*prathamaprāptarajoyoga*) and finally 'old age,' i.e. 'with mature hair' (*paścimavayasi, vṛddhā, paliknī or prājñī*, 2:5.1098).

---

[16] According to Geertz, in Javanese it is nearly impossible to say anything without indicating the social relationship between the speaker and the listener in terms of status and familiarity (Guha 1983, 43).

Other terms double as lexical markers delineating various sub-divisions within a particular domain such as youth, middle age or old age. They also serve as a gloss for age-specific norms, roles, statuses, and expectations that Indian tradition uses to organize every individual's progression through the life course. Gender is another lexical marker in the semantic domain of age. The way in which the attributes of old age are combined is sex-specific. *Jarā*, the most common term for aging as well as old age, for instance, is feminine in gender. Accordingly, aging too receives by association, various attributes (positive or negative) usually reserved for women. It comes to be personified as evil ogress, tigress, or female cat through the device of suggestion.

Vārdhaka, a substantive in neuter gender and denoting 'old-agedness,' on the other hand, is usually free of negative innuendos frequently associated with the female sex in the Buddhist and later Hindu tradition. As it is understood in classical Hindu tradition and its literature the concept of *vārdhaka* is composed of two components: (1) The process of aging which is biological in nature and whose meaning is expressed semantically (*jarā*), and (2) The phenomenon of old age which is a cultural construct and is understood semiotically, that is, with reference to clearly discernible signs (*vārdhakya*).

Aging is one significant domain in life where the problems of meaning and interpretation become particularly acute when a sharp and uneasy awareness of old age in the form of indelible and clear signs on the body and mind dawns on the individual. Old age precipitates a crucial disjunctive experience in the inner life of individuals by confronting them with the psychologically traumatic event of the approaching end. Further, the daily diminishing vitality begins to threaten personal integrity and identity. It would seem strange if these experiences, which occur and recur in the life of the human species, had not been given cultural meaning and objectification through language and literature. Contemporary developments in social linguistics show how language reflects various biases--sexism, racism, and ageism in patterns of communication. The process of coining new words of praise or derision for old people exists in all cultures. Praise words invented for old people are quickly turned the other way--euphemisms such as senior citizen often become laden with a heavy freight of sarcasm.[17]

Since language is the primary code that enables humans (1) to develop and internalize norms which constitute religious tradition and culture and (2) to communicate with each other a variety of inner, personal experiences of reality, the semantic organization of old age encoded in language (Sanskrit in this case) is an essential prerequisite of any study of old age. It is only through a self that can communicate with the world through a shared language that our experience of ourselves and of the surrounding world acquires coherence and meaning. The stages of life and the particular definitions of developments within it, including aging, have no meaningful existence apart from what people make of them in and through their words and deeds. With these observations in mind the present study seeks to answer the following questions:

(1) How are age-related lexemes (*padas*) brought in relation to each other? What rhetorical/formal devices produce a coherent conceptual organization underlying these relationships? (*samarthapadavidhi*)
(2) How does age, along with class and gender (*varṇavayalinga,* see Vakroktijīvita 2:21-23) influence the formation of larger lexical units and markers (*kṛttaddhitasamāsa*), their congruity, and their wider semantic domain in Sanskrit literature?

The intent of this exercise, however, is not to create a thesaurus of terms relating to age but rather to facilitate by commenting on meaningful words, compounds and phrases, elicitation of the attributes, attitudes, and responses toward old age in Sanskrit literature. Lexemes or phrases in Sanskrit texts that are ostensibly used to divide and describe the life course, in fact, also serve as glosses for the deeper levels of meaning. The

---

[17] Donald Cowgill (Holmes et al 1983, 2) has commented on how, once positive references may become abusive through time. The word gaffer, for instance, had originally been a term of respect (a contraction of grandfather), and fogy, in 17th century meant "a wounded military veteran." Codger, which originally was a slang term for meaning "to beg" began being applied to old people in the late 18th century with a connotation of meanness and stinginess. Old women tend to fare worse than old men. Hag, crone, and old maid date back nearly four hundred years, but derogatory terms for elderly men did not appear before about 1800.

way in which the attributes of old age are combined, for instance, is often class and gender specific. They may or may not be sex specific or sexually neutral. Other attributes seem to be more salient for female sex than the male.

Language and meaning in the Indian tradition

The organizing principle for the above task is based on the general theory of meaning first expounded in the Nāṭyśāstra of Bharata and further developed by such later thinkers as Kuntaka, the ninth century rhetorician. According to one modern Indian literary critic, in the whole range of Sanskrit poetical theory, we do not have anyone who can be termed an original aesthetic thinker and a practical literary critic in the modern sense of the term except Kuntaka (Krishnamoorthy 1977: xxxvii).[18] More importantly, our interest in Kuntaka is warranted by the fact that he is concerned equally with the formal and semantic aspects of language.

A word according to Sanskrit poetics is basically a sound but its meaning is attribute (*upādhi*). A text is basically a string of denotative words, but its meaning is what these denotative words in the context of the work combine to suggest (Dhayagude 1984: 21). Textual meaning is not something fixed; it varies form context to context. Each word, when used in a different context, is a different word. But textual meaning is not merely contextual; it depends upon the collocation of words. The possibilities of collocation, however, are limited. According to Sanskrit poetics, words have their primary denotative sense which is based on convention (*sanketa*) and which is immediately understood by all speakers of a language as soon as they are heard. Thus the word *vṛddha* in Sanskrit denotes an elderly person. Such a word, which gives this kind of primary, immediate, and conventional meaning, is a denotative word (*vācakaśabda*) and the denoted sense is called denotation (*abhidhā*). Denotative words have a direct reference to the ideas or things they denote. Sometimes, however, words are used in a sense other than their denoted sense. Thus in a compound *jñānavṛddha* (erudite) the word

---

[18] Kuntaka's work, first pointed out by Mahimabhaṭṭa, is more or less modeled upon the Dhvanyāloka and supplements it by extending its insights by adducing more examples. Kuntaka's theory of *vakratā* is analogous to that of *dhvani* of Ānandavardhana (Krishnamoorthy 1977: xvi).

"*vṛddha*" is used to imply maturity. This kind of meaning is called secondary or indicated sense (*lakṣyārtha*). A word, which gives this kind of meaning, is called *lakṣakaśabda*. The relation between a *lakṣakaśabda* (indicative word) and its sense (*lakṣyārtha*), is called *lakṣaṇā* (literally, indication). The semantic function of *lakṣaṇā* operates under three conditions:

(1) The denoted sense should be inapplicable in the given context (e.g. old age in denoted sense in the above example)
(2) The secondary sense should in some way be connected with the primary sense (as 'maturity' is connected with old age)
(3) In using a word in its secondary sense, the speaker must have some purpose in mind which is other than the denotative sense.

Now the secondary meaning is unmechanical and significant only if there is a conscious purpose behind its use. But how can we know that purpose? Sanskrit poeticians answer that we can know the purpose from their power of suggestion (*vyañjana*) in words. A word which gives rise to a suggested meaning is called suggestive word (*vyañjakaśabda*); the suggested sense is called *vyangārtha*. The relation between a suggested word and its suggested meaning is indeterminate (*aniyatā*). It is not a rule that every word should necessarily have a suggested sense in every context. The suggested sense depends upon the associations of a word in a given context.

What is the denoted meaning of words (such as *vṛddha*) in texts? Does the denoted meaning of a word refer to the individual or to the universal? The grammarian Patañjali postulates that the conventional primary meaning of a word refers neither to the individual nor to the universal, but to the attribute (*upādhi*). All words in a work of literature have their denotative base in langauge which is their link with everyday speech and the condition of their comprehensibility. But they do not remain merely at this denotative base, and if they do, they cannot be a literary work. The poet/writer builds upon the denotative base and the superstructure that is built is what Sanskrit poeticians such as Kuntaka and Ānandavardhana call deviation (*vakratā*) or suggestion (*dhvani*).[19] The analogy of lamp

[19] There is some controversy regarding the exact relationship between these two concepts. According to Krishmoorthy, the two are essentially similar. In fact, Kuntaka's *vakratā* already presupposes the theory of *dhvani* (Krishnamoorthy 1977: xxxvii).

illuminating a jar in dark is used to explain it. The lamp represents stated sense (*vācyārtha*), the jar represents suggested reference (*vyangārtha*), which it illuminates and reveals. The meaning which a poem or a text conveys over and above the statements in it (*vācyārtha*), is the work of the power of suggestion in it. (Rayan1972: 52,182). It has the power to bring the hearer/reader to project himself/herself into that surplus meaning.[20] Abhinavagupta describes this last phenomenon as the gradual interpenetration of the hearer's/reader's self (*ātmānupraveśa*). It is due to the inborn human capacity for feeling that all normal persons have. All feelings leave on our mind deep and subtle impressions (*vāsanās, samskāras*). These lie latent and are stored up in our mind, but in appropriate circumstances they are evoked again and become active (Dhayagude 1984: 21).

Kuntaka defines deviant speech (*vakrokti*) as "a unique and novel way of saying," as opposed to the well-known, usual modes of discourse (Vakroktijīvita [hereafter KV] 1:10). This deviancy, according to him, characterizes both the sound structures of words: in poetry and their meanings (KV 1:18ff). He classifies them into six major types in terms of deviancy: (1) in the arrangement of phonemes; (2) in the use of stem and root (synonyms, modifiers, compound words, gender, verb, etc.; (3) in the use of the terminal part of a word, both nominal and verbal (case, number, person, tense, voice, particles, and indeclinable); (4) in the sentence, which again, is of manifold types; (5) in the topic; and (6) in a whole composition. Of these, some of the varieties and subvarieties pertain to the formal structure of language and others to its semantic content--that is, they relate to non-ordinary ways of presenting ideas.

In the present study we are concerned with the first three types only. Deviancy of the first type, Kuntaka affirms, consists in arranging phonemes in a way that is opposed to the standard modes of speech. It comprises of various kinds of alliteration and chime. Deviancy of the second and third types mainly deals with some special or peculiar uses of morphemes and words and their grammatical structures and relations

[20] It is possible to argue that while the Vedic literature in general opts for the denotative sense of old age (*vācyārtha*), the Upaniṣads, Buddhism and classical Hinduism often engage in the suggested meaning of old age (*vyangārtha*).

(Chari 1990: 135).[21] For Kuntaka form in poetry is something over and above the word-form (*śabda*) and its sense (*artha*). Literature (*sāhitya*) is both word and sense together (KV 1:7). Such a notion of literature as the mutual viability or commensurateness of sound and meaning is dependent upon the Pāṇinian distinction between sound and sense. This duality is taken as axiomatic all through their theorizing about language and literature by Sanskrit critics (Chari 1990: 149).

It is therefore not surprising that the subject of aging and old age tends to generate distitnctive rhetoric and style as well as a way of summoning semantic ingenuity in Sanskrit literature. Even contemporary gerontology generates a specific vocabulary native to it. The abstraction of aging and old age, though often intransigent and elusive, persists across Sanskrit literary history as a semantically specified and occupied zone of utterance. The phonetic form of the word cannot be separated from the sense it carries. Therefore, in poetry [and literature in general], both word and meaning stand in need of an additional something called ornamentation (*alamkaraṇa*) in order to distinguish poetry from ordinary discourse. The word and the meaning together constitute the body of poetry or its gross form (*kāvyaśarīra*), and ornament (understood as technique or poetic form) is its special mode of existence (*kāvyātman*) (Chari 1990: 137). *Alamkāra* includes both the structural and semantic features of language use within its twofold classification of figures of sound and figures of sense. The former covers all varieties of patterning of phonic elements, at both the phonemic (*varṇa*) and the morphemic-syntactic level (*pada* and *vākya*), while the figures of sense accounts for the patterned or deviant expression of the semantic or logical content of words and sentences (Chari 1990: 132).

Indian poetics holds that the form, content and thought of the text are inseparable. The style (*riti*), therefore, is not simply a decorative embellishment upon the subject matter. It becomes the very medium in which the subject matter is turned into text. Style, accordingly, is understood as the means and measure by which the writer further ensures that his/her encoded message is decoded in such a way that the targeted reader not only understands the information conveyed, but also

---

[21] According to Chari, Kuntaka is closer to the methods of the Russian Formalists and the proponents of the Prague school, who take a broader view of the scope of literary style than the descriptive linguist (1990: 136).

shares and responds to the writer's intention behind it. The formal body of poetry also includes the "structure" of the meaning embodied, as distinct from the meaning or logical content (*artha*) itself. For Kuntaka, all secondary or nonliteral modes of prediction, including the 'suggestion' of the *dhvani* theory, fall under the formal aspects of the poetic language. What is called style is the totality of the verbal form plus the semantic mode or the mode of expressing meanings, considered as a formal choice or device; to which Sanskrit critics give the designation 'poetic form' (Chari 1990: 141-42).[22]

The language in which ideas and thoughts are formulated and communicated to others has, as Kuntaka has observed, an important and subtle influence on the style and structure through which thought is inscribed in language as well as its content. The structure of language faithfully reflects the patterns of people's thinking. This partly explains why meaningful responses and reactions to the process of aging and the phenomenon of old age are inscribed in Sanskrit literature through resort to one or more deliberately chosen patterns of style and genre. Put differently, reactions to the consequences of aging and old age, whether interpreted positively or negatively, are enshrined in a particular mode of expression thought to be particularly congenial to that mode. When lexemes are structurally and stylistically organized or compounded in a particular fashion, they clearly encode and control the movements of the borne meaning, providing thereby clues to the way the reader's attention must move in order to recover that meaning. In other words, a given text acquires its meaning and unique identity by virtue of its formal organization and style. When read with close and sensitive attention, the text does not just communicate an inert image of outward reality but also simultaneously shapes the reader's attitude towards it.

To write of aging, old age and death, then, it is not unusual to find that contributors to Sanskrit literature are forced to stretch that language's binding capacity (*bandhas*, for instance, see KV 1:22)--stylistic obligations (*sanketa*), ligatures (*sandhi*), and compounds (*samāsa*) to the limit. Not surprisingly, an inspired and visionary poet with such a clear and transparent verbal texture as Aśvaghoṣa, when required, deliberately

---

[22] Similarly, for Hill (1976: 391) formal regularities of a text take precedence over its meaning. His procedure is to work from the linguistic characteristics to the semantic structure of a poem, the assumption being that formal considerations are logically prior to the fixing of meaning (quoted in Chari 1990: 155).

hazes his poetry with opacity in order to bring out, through his diction (*bandha*), the innate ambiguities of the aging process and death. And a novelist of the calibre of Bāṇa must turn around simple words into long and complicated compounds to achieve the same end. In his Kādambarī, for instance, (1953, 128-29) description of the old sage Jābāli runs into several lines made mostly of compound words.

At the level of rhetoric such a task demands at various times a full array of all possible formal and literary devices (meticulously classified by Kuntaka, see above) on the part of Sanskrit writers--from nominal composition, assonance, and alliteration to simile, metaphor, and myth. Thus, a hortatory proposition or injunction has to be phrased in the optative mood to elicit from the reader a response in terms of doing or agreeing to do the thing or action endorsed by the writer, say of the Dharmaśāstra text. On the other hand, the imperative language of fiat is reduced to mere prediction in the Purāṇas. The Ṛgvedic visionary poet engages in the prayer mode in the celebration and veneration of his/her chosen deity which is expected to grant long and healthy life that will only end in ripe old age. In many hymns of the Atharvaveda, the coercive motive can only be generated by resort to a unique composition of charms and spells. Again, many passages in texts such as the Buddhist Nikāyas or the Yogavāsiṣṭha generate a style which is deliberately paratactic, that is, the presentation proceeds by way of succession rather than subordination. The basic idea, for instance, the loss engendered by old age, is succinctly stated at the beginning of the chapter and then further details are piled up as the text moves along, for emotional content and ornamentation. Occasionally, response to aging may be phrased in the form of pun or wit by word-association (*śleṣa*), which may be understood as simultaneous expression of two or more meanings. The linguistic form underlying two or more meanings may be the same or different. In some verses *every* word has at least two meanings and the composition is, accordingly, two different entities, not one. There are several interesting instances of this ingenuity in verses that seek to relate or somehow accommodate the contrasting norms and ideals of youth and old age.

Modes of expressing age

The foregoing suggests why meaningful responses and reactions to the process of aging and the phenomenon of old age are inscribed in Sanskrit literature by resort to various contrived patterns of style and genre. The internal structure of such texts thereby acquires evocative powers and a peculiar semantic weight. Put differently, semantic shifts in the meaning of aging and old age, whether interpreted positively or negatively, are enshrined in a mode of expression chosen from such formal domains as (1) Nominal composition (2) Optative mood or (3) Assonance

Nominal composition

The function of language, in literature as also in everyday life, is semantic. The most obvious semantic level, as outlined above, is the denotative (*abhidhā*). Meanings of words are fixed at this level strictly by convention (*sanketa*). The dictionary rule "this is the word, this is the meaning (*asmāt padāt ayam artho boddhavyah*) is always valid here (Dhayagude 1984: 235). Even a cursory glance at Sanskrit literary texts reveals that the vocabulary of gerontological significance employed therein revolves around three key Sanskrit verbs: *jṛ*, *vṛdh*, and *vi.*

(1) The verb *jṛ* is by far the most frequently used verb indicating a broad range of age-related meanings. Pāṇini's Dhātupātha illustrates the primary meaning (*upalakṣaṇā*) of *jṛ* as loss due to age (*jṛş vayohanau*, Siddhānta Kaumudī 2:338). Standard Sanskrit dictionaries list five secondary or collocative meanings of *jṛ* with *parasmaipada* endings:

(1) To grow old, wear out, wither away, decay.
(2) To perish, be consumed (also in the figurative sense).
(3) To be dissolved, digested.
(4) To break up or fall to pieces.
(5) As a causative the verb means to make old, wear out, consume or to cause to be digested, to digest.

As *ātmanepada* the verb *jṛ* has two meanings.

(a) To move, approach, come near.
(b) To call out, praise, laud, invoke.

This double sense is evident in one hymn in the Ṛgveda (1:124.10), which addresses the goddess of dawn, Usas, in this manner: O lovely one, thou that awakenest, that causest old age...(*revat stotre sunṛte jarāyanti*). Geldner observes that here, *jarāyanti* has the two-fold sense of awakening and aging. But Bloomfield opines that *jarāyanti* has the added meaning of "causing songs to be sung" because it is after Uşas has dawned that hymns are sung (Venkatasubbiah n.d., 134-36). Similarly, the substantive *jarābodha*, derived from the root *jṛ* (Rg 1:27.10), is of doubtful meaning. While Sāyaṇa's gloss on it refers to one of the possible meanings, i.e. "known through praise," Ludwig holds it to be the name of a seer. Roth regards it as a mere adjective meaning "attending to the invocation," which is perhaps the most probable interpretation. Oldenburg, however, thinks that it is a proper name, the literal sense being "alert in old age." (Macdonnell 1967: 277-78).[23] It is not clear, however, why a verb meaning 'to age' should have developed such a secondary and collocative meaning (assuming that 'to age' *is* its primary meaning) denoting 'to praise.' In view of the clear difference between the two sets of meanings, it may be that the two meanings essentially belong to two homonymous verbs. It is also useful to remember that apart from the Ṛgveda, the secondary meaning of praise is not retained in the post-Vedic literature.

(2) The verb *vṛdh* is illustrated in the Siddhānta Kaumudī in the sense of to grow or increase (*vṛdh vṛddhau*, 2:182). As an *ātmanepada* verb, it connotes two basic meaning: (a) To increase, augment, strengthen and (b) To grow, grow up, increase.

(3) The verb *vi* is illustrated in the sense of to go, pervade, conceive, shine, throw or eat.[24] It is interesting to note that the conjugated forms of the above three verbs are relatively less frequently used in classical Sanskrit literature to denote aging. This need not surprise us since the tendency to accord primacy to the substantive over the verb is well known in post-Vedic Sanskrit literature. Predictably, far more common are compounds and substantives construed on them: *jarā*, *vṛddha* and *vayas* (age, from *vi*). But as the dictionary listings indicate, the formations of such substantives invariably leave them with inherent vagueness of meaning and emotive overtones. Semantic shifts, suggestive of the widening of the original meaning, are evident in many of them.

In Buddhist texts the Pali term *vuddhi* (Sanskrit *vṛddhi*) is used in the sense of the opposite of decay caused by the aging process (*parihāni*). The term is intended to denote spiritual growth, not decay. The inspiring message of the Buddha, then, is to be understood as "people are decaying [aging]; as learners of this *dhamma* (the Buddha's teachings), they will

---

[23] Nirukta (10:8); Pāṇini (3: 3.104); Sāyaṇa on Ṛg 1: 27.10.

[24] Siddhānta Kaumudī 2: 287.

grow." Rhys-Davids (1965 preface, xii) has argued that this usage of the term 'will become,' 'grow' implies not merely 'will be.' 'Become' here is set in opposition to 'decaying' or 'aging,' thus indicating no further 'becoming' in the future, but, rather, a causal process, an evolution. There is such a context, both in the Upaniṣads and Piṭakas, where *bhaviṣyanti* and other conjugations of the verb *bhū* clearly mean more than just a copula or bare future state.

As pointed out above, *abhidhā* is the normal mode but not the norm of expression in a given context. There is no word at this level to describe, for example, the violent or destructive qualities of the aging process. Here the merely denotative use of language fails. As Kuntaka observes, one has to resort to a deviant mode of expression (*vakratā*) to convey the desired extended sense. The deviation consists in using words not in their primary denotative sense but in their secondary associative sense. Thus, to convey the violent, destructive qualities of aging, the Yogavāsiṣṭha describes it by juxtaposing it metaphorically with the expression 'shrieking owl.' Here the text uses the word she-jackal not in its primary sense, i.e. a kind of quadruped, but in its associative sense of scheming, cruel feline etc. The function of language at this semantic level (i.e. associative meanings) is called *lakṣaṇā*. The semantic function of *lakṣaṇā* either extends the meaning of an expression or substitutes an altogether different meaning for it.

Later classical writers profiting from these fundamental ambiguities seem to have succeeded in creating cognitively and emotively synonymous words by resorting to the popular and creative technique of componential compounding. In what follows below, three typical rhetorical devices based on the technique of nominal composition will be examined, viz. formulaic lists, numeral terms, and colour vocabulary to refer to old age. The descriptive determinative type of nominal composition (*karmadhāraya*) based on the juxtaposition of two substantives (one of which usually being *jarā*, *vṛddha* or *vayas*) is also a favourite. Used in similes and metaphors, these compounds enhance and render colour as well as a particular shade of nuanced significance, through the phenomenon of deviation (*vakratā*), to the denoted bare meaning of old age.[25]

[25] Sanskritist G. B. Palsule (1961: 104) remarks that the present set of meanings attributed to Sanskrit verbs was not originally a part of the Pāṇinian Dhātupāṭha. It is the

The Amarakośa explicitly links old age with decrepitude (*visrasā jarā* 2:6.40). Lingyasūrin's gloss, in explaining *visrasā*, attributes the eventual falling apart (or breaking down) of the body to old age (*viśramsate adhah patati śarīiram anayeti viśrasā*). Mallinātha's explanation of this definition is that old age refers to the ripening of the body caused by the final [phase of] age (*caramavayah kṛtaśarīraparipāka nāmani*). As a feminine substantive *jarā*, has come to mean decrepitude, infirmity and general debility consequent on old age.[26] Secondarily, it denotes digestion or greeting. In later mythology it is the name of a female demon.

Compounds featuring *jarā* as one of the basic semantic units are comparatively rare in Vedic literature. The exocentric compound *jardastih* (one having attained old age) occurs frequently in the Ṛgveda.[27] *Jarāmṛtyu* as an exocentric compound (*bahuvrīhi*) occasionally occurs in the Atharvaveda where it is construed to mean one dying in old age or dying due to old age.[28] This reflects the generally positive appreciation of old age in the Vedic society where people expressed an eager desire to live long enough to enjoy life even in old age.

In the Upaniṣads, however, old age begins to acquire an extended and wider connotation, which is negative and pejorative in character. The

---

work of post-Pāniṇian grammarians such as Bhīmasena and others. Further, the particular meanings were never regarded as exhaustive. They were always open to additions from time to time in accordance with the actual usage of the language. This is reflected in the early acceptance of the doctrine that verbs possess various meanings (*dhatunām anekārthatva*).

[26] The substantive *jarā* is formed by adding the suffix *an* to the verbal base *jṛ* according to Pāṇini 3:3.104 (*vayohānau* with *sidbhidadibhyo'n*). It is then augmented on the basis of Pāṇini 7: 4.16 (*rdṛṣo'ni guṇah*). The feminine suffix *ṭāp* is then added following Pāṇini 4: 1.4 (*ajadyataṣṭāp*). Pāṇini (7: 2.101) rules that optionally *jaras* may be substituted for *jarā* (*jarayā jarasanyatarasyām iti jarasādeśah*). The Kāśikā on this rule, as explained in Limaye (1974: 644-645), is that the substitution is warranted by the succeeding *aja vibhakti (jarā ityetasya jaras ityayamādeśo bhavati anyatarasyām āadau vibhaktau paratah*). Thus, one may express the phrase, "teeth fall on account of old age" in Sanskrit either as *jarasā dantāh śīryante* or as *jarayā dantāh śīryante.*

[27] Consider, for instance, the occasion when the groom says to his bride: *Gṛhṇāmi te saubhagtvāya hastam mayā patyā jaradaṣṭiryathasah* (Ṛg 10:85.36). Sāyaṇa glosses the compound *jaradaṣṭih* to mean one having attained old age.

[28] See Atharvaveda 12:3.55; 19:24.4,8; 19:26.1; 2:13.2; 2:28.2,4; 8:2.11.

term *jarāmṛtyu*, for instance, is now construed as a co-ordinative compound to mean old age *and* death. Old age is thereby equated or elevated to the status of death and is equally feared. It also occurs in early Buddhism. In his Buddhacarita (4:89), for instance, Aśvaghoṣa often construes exocentric compounds based on *jarā* and/or *mṛtyu* to convey similar meanings: one characterized by death, disease and decrepitude (*mṛtyuvyādhijarā dharmah*); he has Siddhārtha declaring that "having known the fear of old age and death, I have given myself to this discipline" [of ascetic life.] (*aham jarā mṛtyubhayam viditvā mumukṣāya dharmam imam prapannah* BC 11:7). Elsewhere the Buddha is described as the one who put an end to birth and old age (*janmajarāntakah* 3:1). In the classical Sanskrit literature, which features numerous compounds based on *jarā/ajarā*, similar negative appreciation of old age, first initiated in the Upaniṣadic period, is retained.[29]

The substantive *vṛddha* and compounds based on it, by contrast, tend to depict old age or elderly persons in a relatively more favourable light.[30] Though somewhat rare in the Vedic literature, in classical texts they are more commonly used collocatively in the sense of increased, augmented; full grown, grown up; advanced in years; wise, learned; eminent in; and diṣti nguished by. As a masculine substantive, *vṛddha* carries a meaning a worthy, honorable man; a sage, saint; a male descendent.[31] Thus, old

---

[29] Similar semantic shifts in the meaning of old age are discernible in copmpounds such as: *jarātura*: infirm, old, ill on account of age; *jarāpariṇata*: bent with age; *jarābhiru*: afraid of old age, (also an epithet of the god of love Madana); *jarāśīla*: having old age as a characteristic mark; *jarālakṣman*: sign of old age; *jarādharma*: a particular duty to be performed in old age; *jaratviṭa*: old jester; *jaratkuṭṭtaṇī*: old procuress. In Raghuvamśa (18:7) King Nabha of the Raghu dynasty is said to have gone to the forest to "age with the deer." The commentary explains this to mean that the King bound himself to the task of attaining liberation.

[30] Thus the commentator of Raghuvamśa (1:22) explains old age to be of two kinds: (1) attributable to knowledge; and (2) to the process of aging.

[31] The Amarakośa (2:6.42) furnishes following synonyms of old man (*vṛddha*)

pravayah: one who has gone beyond the age of youth.
sthavirah: one who has "stood" a long time.
vṛddha: one who has grown with age.
jīrṇah: one who loses due to age.
jaran: one who is aging.

Vidura, a cousin of the blind King Dhṛtarāṣṭra, is described in the Udyoga Parvan of the Mahābhārata as *prajñāvayovṛddha* (2:18) or *vṛddha prajñah* (33:53) i.e. ditinguished by discriminating wisdom by using descriptive determinative compound (*karmadhāraya*).

The composition of compounds based on the substantive *vayas* derived from the verb *vi* appears to be a classical phenomenon wherein the extended meaning of *vayas* refers to advancing age or the phase in life. Other secondary meanings of *vayas* include youth, prime of life or any other period or stage in life.[32] This sense is apparent in many compounds built on *vayas*:

> *vayahpariṇati*: ripeness of age
> *vayahpramāṇa*: measure or duration of age
> *vayahsamdhi*: life juncture.

With other relevant and appropriate words, *vayas* is further compounded to indicate any phase in the human life cycle:

> *navamvayah*: young
> *vayogata*: advanced in age
> *caturthavayasah*: very old, in the fourth [final] phase of life.

Nominal composition built on numeral base

Certain age-sensitive compounds construed on a numeral base often acquire symbolic value in relation to aging. Investigations in structural anthropology dealing with numbers and their cultural significance in the fields of music, folklore, religion, and syntax suggest that a definite number inherently characterizes certain things and events. In many traditional societies such as India's, identity of numbers is believed to represent the very *essence* of a given thing or idea. Cultivating insight into

---

vayaśrīyan: one who is extremely old.
daśami: one who is above the age of ninety
(Literally, in the tenth decade).

[32] The formation of such compounds describing a particular age group is based on Pāṇini 3: 2.10 (*vayasi ca*).

unique numerical relations is said to enable the wise to detect hidden meanings and relations among things, events and phenomena.

A Ṛgvedic hymn to the twin gods Aśvins (1:34) is composed on the numerical motif of three (*Dreizahl*). In the course of twelve verses the number three, which is invested with esoteric significance, is evoked thirty-six times! This well known predilection of the Indians for classifications, groupings and enumerations invested with specific metaphysical or esoteric meanings, already evident in the Vedic literature, grows more obsessive in the later classical period. Compounds involving low numerals such as *trivarga* (set or class of three items) and *catuṣṭaya* (group of four values or propositions) are common in classical Sanskrit texts. Figures such as twenty-five, fifty, seventy-five, hundred or even thousand are imbued with sacred, mystic meanings and appear in numerous passages of gerontological significance. Ṛgvedic prayers and Atharvan charms, where the concern is with a long healthy life, employ these numbers for their allegedly esoteric or magical potential.

As Gonda (1976: 94-95) explains, the correspondence between the ritual act or fact, *in casu* the ritual triad and the tripartite universe, is believed to enable the officiating priest to exert considerable influence. The human body and its life processes are also believed to have unique numeric correspondences and as such are amenable to divine or priestly/magical intervention. Thus the three seasons in the year are identical with the three vital breaths animating the human body (Śatapatha Brāhmaṇa 12: 3.2.1); the medical skill of the Aśvins is deposited in equal proportions in three places--in fire (*agni*), in water (*apas*) and in Brahmin. In practicing medicine, therefore, the three should be near at hand (Taittirīya Samhitā 6:4.9.2., see also chapter five dealing with the rejuvenation therapy where this Vedic directive is respected). Occasionally, the sense of old age is also contrived in terms of a mass or numeric substantive, e.g. *atijīrṇa* (very old) or *aśitīka* (in the eighth decade [of life]).

The number one hundred figures in numerous formalized and stylized expressions and denotes 'many.' Such is the case in hymns from the Ṛgveda (10: 162.3) or the Atharvaveda (3: 11.3,4,5) where long life stretching to one hundred autumns (*śarādahs*) is requested. Sāyaṇa in his comments on these verses, points out that expressions such as *śatam* (hundred) and *sahasram* (thousand) are to be understood as meaning *aparimitānām* (boundless) or *bahunām* (numerous) and not literally. In Yajurveda (3: 62), long life stretching to three life spans (*tryayuṣām*) is asked. Similar usage is also reported in the medical texts in the rejuvenation and revitalization prescriptions where a life span of thousands of years is guaranteed to the users. By contrast, in the Dharmaśāstra literature, the number one hundred is used to represent a specific quantitative measure of time in which human life is lived.

Nominal composition in formalized lists

Long, co-ordinative compounds frequently figure in many highly codified, stylized and formalized lists of objects or persons of varying dispositions or stations and ritual status in life.[33] They are designed to effect precise semantic shifts in order to widen the meaning and enhance nuanced shades of meaning of expressions wherein they occur.Old men and/or women frequently appear in these listings where they share one or more traits in common with the other people on the list. These groupings tend to be optimally homogeneous with certain shared similarities and psychological proximities. Often each member of the compound may be handicapped by one or the other weakness or deficiency of a physical, psychological or emotional nature. Or they all may be deemed to be worthy of respect or honour on account of services rendered in the past. The presence or absence of old persons in such groupings, therefore, constitutes important sources and clues to our understanding the meaning of the aging process.

A passage dealing with the duties of a householder Yājñavalkya counsels him not to squabble with certain types of persons in order to maintain peace and harmony in the household. The list includes persons such as: one's parents, guests, brothers, in-laws, members of maternal uncle's family, elderly, young ones, sick individuals, preceptors, physicians, and so on (Ysm 1: 6.157-58). Elsewhere he advices the couple to dine on the leftovers after the young people, young married women, elderly folks, pregnant women, sick people, girls, itinerant guests and the servants have been fed (Ysm 1: 5.105). But in a section dealing with the mundane matters (*vyavahāra*), Yājñavalkya cautions that elderly persons make

---

[33] Manu prescribes a series of syntactic variations on a string of compound words to make elderly wanderers (*sanyāsins*) identify themselves by their respective class affiliations (*varṇas*) while calling for alms (MS 2:49). Similarly, among acquaintances phatic statements about each other's health must include the word *kuśala* if addressed to a Brāhmaṇa, *anāmaya* to a Kṣatriya, *kṣema* to a Vaiśya, and *anārogya* to a Śudra (MS 2: 127) (Guha 1983: 42).

unreliable witnesses. So are for that matter, women, children, actors, heretics, handicapped and thieves (Ysm 2: 5.70). At another place in the same text the list is comprised of women, old men, gamblers, drunkards, mad men, persons who are defamed, and actors or heretics (Ysm 1: 2.72,73). In a section on ordeals he admonishes: women, children, elderly, the blind, the handicapped, the Brahmins and the sick are to be prescribed a "balance ordeal" which does not involve physical punishment or torture. The formation of such lists suggests that the elderly, women, children and the sick share the general trait of vulnerability, and for that purpose they are grouped together.

Colour vocabulary

Vedic Indians were already sensitized to contrasts of light and dark. They tended to describe as light or dark things which were contrasted or opposed for other reasons, but which cannot be considered definitely white or black. The dark and light contrast in Vedic poetry also came to reflect a contrast between death and life, night and day, and old and young.

Toward the period when the Brāhmaṇa texts were compiled (ca.800 BCE), the opposition was extended to include bright, immortality, life, youth and moisture, on the one hand, and dark, mortality, death, old age and dryness, on the other.[34] Moisture and warmth sustain life; their opposites cause death. The living creature is by nature moist and warm, and to live is to be such. But old age is cold and dry, and so is what is dead. It is inevitable; therefore, that one who grows old should dry up. This line of interpretation is also found in the classical Sanskrit literature where people are described, as if they were plants, in terms of their moisture content or dryness.

In the Raghuvamśa of Kālidāsa (3:32) the growing up of the young Raghu is compared to the shooting forth/sprouting of the bamboo stalk. On the contrary, old people like dry or rotten leaves, stems and stumps of trees, turn pale or yellow. The following simile from the Yogavāsiṣṭha suggests that meaning:

---

[34] Mahābhārata (Śānti 271.33) echoes this thought claiming that the fate of the soul is related to its colour. The soul may have one of the six colours--white, yellow, red, blue, grey and black. White is the most excellent colour, black is the worst.

> The more the body approaches ripeness and decline, so much more does death rejoice in it. The body grows lean with grey hair on the head just as a creeper, having flowered, fades away (1:27.4).

Writers of Sanskrit texts also make use of a number of compounds involving a relevant colour term to designate a particular age-bracket and the physical condition of that person. The number of such compounds is high, since Sanskrit has a large number of synonyms for each of the seven colours of the solar spectrum. The Amarakośa lists fourteen terms to denote the colour white. Some of the more commonly used terms for white are: *śukla, śubhra, gaura, dhavala* and *pāṇdura* (1: 5.12,13). The colour black can be expressed in terms of seven different words--*kṛṣṇa, nīla, asita, śyāma* and *kāla* being the more frequently used (1:5.14). When Baudhāyana, compiler of the Dharmasūtra text named after him, admonishes that the Śruti texts enjoin the dark-haired person to offer sacrifice to the god Agni (BDS 1:2.6), he understands the term dark-haired one (*kṛṣṇakeśah*) to mean a householder, that is, one who is in his/her middle age. The implication is that one who is (not dark-haired = old) should not keep the sacred fire. Such a one must renounce the world.

Palita (grey, see Amarakośa 2:6.40)35 is a common term of reference used to describe anyone in his/her middle age.36 Lingyasūrin notes that the basic meaning of the verb *pal* is in the sense of movement. But because of the polyvalent nature of the Sanskrit verbs, it also means adorn. He then points out one meaning of *palitam* as that whereby the charm of the body is enhanced on account of the white [hair due to old age]. *Palitam*, thus, is a term referring to the greying of the hair due to old age. By extending the analogy further the formation of a compound such as *pakvakeśyā* (one with ripe hair) is explained as a synonym of (woman with ripe, grey hair). The classical Sanskrit literature is replete with such descriptive

[35] Derived from the verb *pal*, (class 1 with the *parasmaipada* ending), it is irregularly formed with the addition of the *itac* suffix according to the rule outlined in the Uṇādi Sūtra (3: 92). Patanjal (1963: 192), on the basis of Uṇādi Sūtra 5: 34 cites another illustration (*phal niṣpattau*) from the Dhātupātha and explains the formation of the term *palita* as that which ripens.

[36] *Paliknī* is a synonym for old woman, which Lingyasūrin's gloss on Amarakośa 2:6.12 explains as on account of [her] grey hair, *palitaromayogāt*.

determinative compounds coined to describe persons approaching old age. By way of example, one may cite the following:

> *palitadarśanam*: appearance of grey [hair]
> *palitabhaviṣṇu*: becoming grey
> *palitabhāvuka*: turning grey

The term grey with reference to hair indicates middle age. For purely cognitive reasons, similes employing age-sensitive colour vocabulary are stored and recycled for properties or characteristics that are difficult to describe digitally, that is, based on the presence or absence of individual attributes. Certain age-specific colours such as white, grey or black, therefore, are learned and stored in analogic fashion. The concept of blackness, in a gerontological context, is necessarily tied to statements such as, "the colour of hair in young age is black," or "the colour of hair is grey in middle age." Such use of a distinct colour vocabulary with respect to aging is prevalent in most cultures (as illustrated by a citation from the Baudhāyana Dharmasūtra above), because the meaning of old age cannot be analyzed into sets of attributes, but must instead be illustrated with literary devices such as similes or metaphors.

A classical Sanskrit text discussing canons of arts lays down the convention that spatial directions, when represented in painting, should be depicted as women belonging to different age groups. The south, for instance, is to be portrayed as a young girl with a golden hue and seated in a chariot. The West is to be shown as a mature woman of dark complexion and riding a horse. The North-West is to be shown as being blue in colour and approaching old age (*āsannapalita nīlā vadavā*). The North is to be shown as an old woman astride a man. The North-East is to be shown as very old with pale skin and seated on a bull.

Nominal composition is also used to group persons of different class status in a ritually significant hierarchical order. A well-known Pāṇinian rule (2:2.34) is interpreted in such a way as to make the words standing for the four *varṇas* replicate the *varṇa* hierarchy itself in a compound of the co-ordinative (*dvandva*) class and put them together in their ascriptive order descending from Brāhmaṇa to Śūdra.[37]

---

[37] The *sūtra* "*alpachatram*" of Pāṇini (2:2.34) has a *vārttika* laying down that "the castes are placed according to their order" (*varṇānām anupūrvyena pūrvanipātah*) so that the

Optative mood

In addition to nominal composition, another effective formal device of controlling or moving meaning in the intended direction that is frequently used in the Dharmaśāstra texts is to use the optative or imperative mood (*vidhirling*). By effectively resorting to this device, a text such as the Manusmṛti has invested Indian society with a well-developed and explicit ideal model of living out one's life cycle. It divides the ideal life span of hundred years into a sequence of four distinct phases punctuated or marked by appropriate rituals. Detailed instructions as to how the members of each class (*varṇa*) are to live are phrased in the form of moral precepts or phrases in the optative mood.

Technically these statements are known as *vidhi* (injunction). A *vidhi* is usually a particular duty that is incumbent upon an individual by virtue of being born in a particular class (*varṇa*), age (*vayas*) and gender (*linga*). A duty is couched in the form of an injunction, because it is not likely to be instinctively or spontaneously fulfilled by the individual in question in terms of his/her class, age and gender. *Vidhi*, therefore, has the same significance as in the Talmudic literature the *halakah* has for the Jews; it is simply authoritative.

Passages dealing with old age and aging may be fruitfully analyzed for their semantic content on the basis of the science of interpretation developed by Jaimini in his Pūrva Mīmāmsā system. Thus, a promising statement may be examined to determine whether it is phrased in a *vidhi* or *arthavāda* form on the hypothesis that semantic meaning is generated and controlled with resort to a particular mood. *Vidhi*, for instance, is an injunction declaring a duty that is not likely to be instinctively or spontaneously fulfilled by an individual. A statement such as "having been a householder, let one leave for a forest" is a *vidhi* statement commonly found in the Dharmaśāstra texts, which asks the aging individual to renounce home and enter the forest as a hermit, an act he/she is unlikely to undertake on his/her own.

---

rule governing combination in a *dvandvasamāsa* according to the relative weight of syllables would not apply in this particular instance--The compound would then read *brāhmaṇakṣatriyaviśaśūdrāh* (Vasu 1891, 273-74 Pāṇini Aṣṭādhyāyī). Guha wryly observes that this is a clear case of ideology moulding grammar in its own image (1983: 43).

An injunction is intended to instigate an individual to commit a particular type of action (*kārakahetu*). By contrast, *arthavāda* generally serves as an explanatory or illustrative statement seeking to facilitate or amplify the understanding of an injunction and its execution. Often it may guarantee the fruits resulting from the commission of a particular injunction in a very tempting form so as to lure the sceptical or the recalcitrant person into action. Accordingly, many rejuvenation prescriptions guarantee a life of ten thousand years or even more to any individual who will undergo that particular therapy. *Arthavāda*, then, generally elaborates a *jñāpakahetu* (informative purpose) of a *vidhi* statement. Occasionally, rewards arising out of the performance of a particular duty are put in a very tempting form of *arthavāda* so as to lure the individual into obeying the *vidhi*. Examples of this type of *arthavāda* statements are to be found in the classical medical literature in passages dealing with the rejuvenation (*rasāyana*) therapy where the patient is promised a life of ten thousand years provided he (the therapy is restricted to the male twice-born [*dvija*] only) also cultivates prescribed ethical virtues.

The Yājñavalkyasmṛti, perhaps because of its deeper this-worldly commitment or orientation, employs a somewhat different and more elaborate scheme to inscribe its own meaning of the class and stage-bound duties (*varṇāśramadharma)*. In the process it furnishes us with materials of much gerontological relevance. Under the category of *varṇadharma*, for instance, it is laid out that the stage of renunciation (*sanyāsa*) is to be entered by the elderly male ideally at the age of seventy-five.

A scrutiny of the *dharma*-related duties as prescribed in the Dharmaśāstras, therefore, is likely to prove a valid source of information regarding the attitude toward old age in traditional Indian society. It also indicates how the Dharmaśāstra writers clothe their thoughts in varied linguistic modalities in order to avail themselves of different types of nominal compositions, phrases and grammatical means to express many delicate semantic distinctions and gradations in their treatment of old age and aging. In their hands Sanskrit develops into a delicately tuned language able to acknowledge the differing statuses both in vocabulary and tone. One is instructed to use different forms of address for the oldest and the older relation. Nor is this kind of distinction limited to one's own generation. An uncle older than one's father is addressed differently than one's father's younger brother.

Another interesting feature of this particular formal mode is that since brahminical social linguistics and ethics is generally couched in injunctive statements, negation is an exception. Early Buddhism, on the other hand, is fascinated by negative expressions. Love for the negative approach is so great in Buddhism that its highest goal *nirvāṇa*, wherein the triple evil of old age, disease and death is absent, is given a negative appellation. Ethical virtues that the monks are exhorted to cultivate are also couched in negative terms (*niṣedhas*).

Assonance

As discussed above, for Kuntaka, the question whether the sound properties of words are in any way related to meaning, whether they affect meaning at all, and how they affect meaning is a stylistic or rather, formal consideration.[38] Sound structures are not directly expressive of meanings and do not affect meaning, they can nevertheless play an evocative or heightening role in literary expression. Their function is determined by the semantic context in which they occur and is dependant on it (Chari 1990: 153).[39] The formal mode of assonance is principally comprised of rhyme and alliteration deliberately produced to elevate the diction of the verse to reach the lofty heights of ideas such as those expressed in Ṛgveda 1:124.1)

> Without violating the divine ordinances, reducing the ages of man, Uṣas has shown forth as the last of many who have passed by, as the first of those who are to come (Gonda's translation 1973: 51).

Alternatively, the essential ideas or their inter-relationships may be expressed by producing short, stylized phrases such as *śaradah śatam* (one hundred year lifespan) or *puruṣam purātanam* (to the old man)

---

[38] Hymes (1960) has argued that the nexus between sound and language is not quite so arbitrary as it is made out to be but a phenomenon to be reckoned with. He tries to demonstrate by his analysis of a number of English sonnets that there is congruence between sounds and meanings that can be objectively analyzed (cited in Chari 1990: 151).

[39] Consider, in this context, Olson's observation (1980: 102) that Ricoeur finds the standard taxonomic and semantic analyses of metaphor less than completely adequate. Indeed, it is not until metaphor is better understood as a figure of deviation within the structure of a complete phrase or sentence that its nature can be more fully comprehended.

which occur frequently in many Vedic texts. Two words or vocables which sound alike but mean different things may also be brought together to produce a double effect upon the ear and mind of the listener. Though etymologically cognate, these words do not generally convey even distantly related meanings. To the casual listener, however, this is not always or immediately clear. A very pertinent example, as pointed out above, is the use of the Vedic verbal root *jṛ* meaning to age and also to praise. While classical Sanskrit has retained only the first meaning, instances are not lacking in the Ṛgveda where both these meanings are juxtaposed in the same verse.

Words with unique sounds are so arranged in some of the didactic tracts as to generate lexical congruity. Alliterated pairs of words or expressions may also be made to reverberate with one another. The Taittirīya Brāhmaṇa occasionally (3:7.7.3) contains expressions such as 'may we live long till old age.' Gonda (1959: 196) points out the wide distribution of compounds both parts of which alliterate is indication of the popularity of this technique, e.g. *samsāra sāgara* (sea of transmigration), *jarā jarjarā* (impeded by old age). The binding and associative force of alliteration, particularly when the words involved are semantically related (e.g. *jīrnaśīrna* or *jarā jarjarā* where both indicate decrepitude), help reinforce an association of meaning and ideas. The lexical congruity so created is then made to stretch across the entire verse or the passage producing an integrative structure of interlacing syntax, alliteration and meaning so that when the text or the passage thus arranged is read aloud, it produces a magical or emotive impression on the hearer or reader. This practice is quite in keeping with Indian poetics which accords an important function to alliterated sound sequences (*śrtyānuprāsa*). Such a combination of powerful and formulaic utterances is thought to be an effective means of enhancing the didactic quality of the composition's recital.

The following examples from the Mohamudgara (The Hammer Striking at Delusion), a popular didactic tract in twelve verses attributed to Śankara, are selected from that text reproduced in Mahadevan (1980, 33-37) by way of illustration:

angam galitam palitam mundam daśanavihitam jātam tundam
vṛddho yāti gṛhitvā daṇdam tadapi na muñcatyāśāpindam

With a sunken body, bent head and a toothless mouth, the aged walks with a staff but does not give up desire (#6).

yāvadvittopārjanasaktas tāvannijaparivāro raktah
paścāj jīvati jarjarā dehe vārtām ko'pi na pṛchati gehe

One's close family members keep the bonds of attachments so long as one is bent on earning money. But no one cares to inquire when one languishes in an infirm body (#5).

bālastāvatkrīdāsaktas taruṇastāvattaruṇiraktah
vṛddhastāvac cintāsaktah pare brahmaṇi ko'pi na saktah.

As a boy one is attached to play; in one's youth, the attachment is to a young woman; in old age one is preoccupied with worries; but alas, no one is committed to transcendent *brahman* (#7).

In verse number six, the last word in each line contains the harsh sounds of n and d, which occur in a definite pattern and rhythm. Their congruity of sounds hovers and reverberates in the mind of the hearer simultaneously creating a realistic image of an old man before the inner eye. Because of their lexical congruity, they touch the audience to the quick. Moreover, they are delightful to the ears and minds of the hearers and speakers because they meet the psychical needs of uniformity and harmony. Being suggestive and fascinating, they can easily establish associations not only between the parts of utterances but also between the persons speaking through these texts and those listening or reading them.

Thus, in the peculiarities pertaining to sound (*śabdacitra*), much ingenuity is displaced in the arrangement of letters, or in the combination of letters making different words or senses. The verbal figures of speech, on which this depends, are broadly speaking, alliteration (*anuprāsa*) and chime (*yamaka*). The former is of two kinds: the alliteration of letters (*varṇāuprāsa*), and the alliteration of words (*padānuprāsa*). In alliteration, there is recurrence of *ṇa* and *da* letters on the one hand, and even of a group of letters, construed as xxx, on the other, intensifying the striking verbal expression produced by the repetition of a regular group of sounds, *nibhṛta* (Jha 1975: 45).

In the works of Kālidāsa and Aśvaghoṣa such rhyming phrases and combinations of sounds are of frequent occurrence. The congruity of sounds at the end of a pair of closely associated works in the first instance makes the listener believe that they express one single and related idea. The similarity in sound tends to transform the meanings of the two components of these phrases into a single new semantic unit. In the above examples from the Ṛgveda and Mohamudgara, one may easily notice the rhythmic sequence of: (1) *ti-ni ti-ni, nam-nam* and (2) *muṇdam-tuṇdam, daṇdam-piṇdam* respectively.

Deliberate duplication of sounds or phrases may be intended to convey reiteration and distribution in space and time. In Sanskrit the locative case is frequently used for such purpose especially when the 'sphere' is a particular point in place or time. For this reason, in the Ṛgveda, expressions such as *yuge-yuge* (in every age) or *gātre-gātre* (in every organ or member of the body) are frequent. Such exclamatory repetitions as *jarā-jarā* (old age, old age), which are put in the mouth of the frightened Siddhārtha who for the first time in his life has come across an old man, in the Buddhacarita of Aśvaghoṣa (3:39) are not merely ornaments. This type of emotional repetition of address or exclamation under the influence of fear, fright or the desire to be heard by others is common in Indian literature.

Many ritual formulae, charms, spells and incantations in the Atharvaveda contain certain stock phrases or syntactic units which appear at the beginning or the end of the verse. These are intended to produce and intensify the magical effect and potency of that particular charm. In one Atharvan prayer to the sun god (Sūrya), the poet enjoins the god to grant him a life of hundred years; the plea is repeated eight times with each phrase ending in the refrain *śaradah śatam* (one hundred autumns). Sometimes, such repetitive phrases are intended to convey the determination and finality of a particular action contemplated. When a hermit has completed his *vānaprastha* stage and feels that he is ready to enter the final stage of the wanderer (*sanyāsin*), he performs a designated rite in the course of which he reiterates his firm resolve to renounce the world by thrice repeating the phrase, *sanyastam mayā* (I have renounced).

Often a structural symmetry between phrases is resorted to in order to present a particular semantic message through highlighted contrasts or parallel actions. The meaning of the poetic message as structured form is construed by positing symmetry between sound and meaning. An interesting example of this practice is found in the *Raghuvamśa* 8:22 where Kālidāsa highlights the contrast between the diverging preoccupations of the retiring old king and his young son who has assumed the responsibilities of the state:

> Neither the youthful king (*nava*=new, young), remaining steadfast in his pursuits till they bore fruit, desisted from acts nor did the old king (*navetara*= other than new, i.e. old), steadfast in discriminating wisdom, cease from the performance of yogic practices before the realization of the supreme self.

To Kālidāsa then, the systematic poetic form is not merely an unfolding of parallel structures of sound and meaning, but a process in which such parallel structural forms serve to create a specific meaning of old age (Tilak 1989: 11).

Kşemendra, the tenth century poet and satirist from Kashmir too, demonstrates a natural inclination to describe contrasting activities in terms of involved parallelisms. Consider following couplet from his Kadaryavarṇanam (2:36) where structural symmetry is resorted to in order to highlight contrasts in the ideals and attitudes held by different types of people: The fool hoards wealth; deluded by greed of profit. The ascetic wastes his beauteous form by restraining the desire of senses.

By skilfully employing various formal modes Sanskrit literary texts seek to capture the unknown and elusive and shape the awareness of the trans-empirical meaning of human reality. For this purpose they superimpose a particular suggested meaning upon the ordinary, denoted and observable physical signs of aging on the body (metonymy). In searching for the meaning of aging as inscribed in the texts under scrutiny in this study, therefore, one must begin by neither devaluing nor ignoring any of the modes through which Sanskrit literary texts struggle to capture the truth of the aging process. They are to be recognized as so many ciphers and keys, as it were, to possible meanings to the queries, "Where does aging and old age fit in the meaning system of the ideal life cycle? What is the value of aging in the ideal scheme of human existence invested with meaning?"

The foregoing suggests that by judicious use of the formal mode of inscribing meaning, Sanskrit literary texts securely locate the meaning and significance of aging and old age where it belongs--in the human body and the mind as circumscribed by the lifespan and in the heart of the lived experience, which somehow also transcends the purely physical dimension. The lexemes and literary expressions that indicate aging in these texts are not a random collection, but rather are structured in terms of an identifiable model that is implicit in the semantics of Sanskrit language. They also suggest that aging is not just an amorphous or porous feeling, but rather that it has an elaborate cognitive structure. They are contrived to furnish a number of nuances and shades of meaning as to what aging is about. It is essential to recognize these interlocking semantic structures evident in various compound formations, use of specific moods, metaphors and myths. Thus merely locating and analyzing all the occurrences of the aging-related words, expressions and modes in Sanskrit literature cannot understand the meaning/s of aging. They must be juxtaposed in a structural relationship to the relevant physical and metaphysical concepts in order to squeeze out, as it were, the hidden meanings operating at the semantic level (Tilak 1989:153).

Chapter 4

Vignettes of old age in Aśvaghoṣa's Buddhacarita and Saundarananda [Shrinivas Tilak]

Aśvaghoṣa

Aśvaghoṣa (ca. 100) was perhaps the first and most important figure who consciously promoted Sanskrit as a spiritual and cultural *lingua franca* in the ancient Indian world. Early Buddhist scriptures were composed and preserved in Pali and other Prakrit languages. Soon texts were also being composed in what is known as hybrid Sanskrit. With Aśvaghoṣa began the trend and practice of using elegant, Pāṇinian Sanskrit as a medium of both verbal and written communication. In the process, he changed the destiny of both Sanskrit and Buddhism by initiating a process of acculturation that centuries later found an echo in the process known today as Sanskritization.

What is eually remarkable is the fact that Aśvaghoṣa had a keen insight into the biological process of aging and the phenomenon of old age which is a cultural construct. In his literary works he skilfully employs the idiom of metaphor to render his understanding of old age accessible to the general public. To elucidate this facet of Aśvaghoṣa thought below I have drawn largely upon *Aśvaghoṣa : a critical study of his authentic Kāvyas, and the apocryphal works, with special reference to his contributions to the classical Sanskrit literature, and his doctrinal standpoint as a Buddhist* by Biswanath Bhattacharya (1976) and *The Buddhacarita or Acts of the Buddha* edited by E. H. Johnston (1972). While I have relied on these works for translation of select Sanskrit passages, I have also modified them to bring out their gerontological significance

Born in a traditional brāhmaṇa family of Saketa near Ayodhya in the modern state of Uttar Pradesh in India, Aśvaghoṣa was attached to the court of King Kaniṣka at Puruṣapura in the first century CE. Formally trained in the sacred Vedic lore as well as in such secular branches of knowledge as grammar and *kāvya*, Aśvaghoṣa's deep knowledge of Sāmkhya, Yoga, and Vedānta has led scholars to believe that he may have become a brāhmaṇa-śramaṇa at one time in his career. It is ovbious that Aśvaghoṣa's intended audience originates in circles in which Brahminical learning and ideas were well known and respected. His references to Brahmins personally and to their institutions are phrased with resepct, and his mythological parallels are drawn from Brahminical sources.

Rahul Samkrtyana, a noted Indian scholar, suggests that in his youth Aśvaghoṣa was involved in a tragic love affair with a girl of Greek origin, forcing the love-lorn poet into a recluse (*śramaṇa)*. Though this is an interesting anecdote without concrete historical evidence, statements of psychological and philosophical nature confronting the youth to its antithesis, i.e. old age, which are discernible in Aśvaghoṣa's works do seem to indicate some such experience and psychological conflict in him.

What is more certain is the fact that at some time in his career he was formally converted to the faith of the Buddha. Aśvaghoṣa's knowledge of his new faith embraced all branches and his spiritual attainments extended, according to Hsuen Tsang, to Śrāvakayāna, Pratyekabuddhayāna, and Bodhisattvayāna. The emphasis on yogic exercises prescribed for and observed by Nanda in Saundarananda are also testimony to Aśvaghoṣa's understanding of the bodhimārga indicating experiential knowledge of this discipline.

Buddhacarita

Buddhacarita is Aśvaghoṣa's first major work and chronologically the earliest. It is an elegant synthesis of historical events in the life of the Buddha and legendary material that grew around his personality in later centuries. To that extent it is comparable to such other biographical works as the Lalitavistara and Mahāvastu. The plot of the Buddhacarita, which begins with the birth of the Buddha and ends with his *mahāparinirvāṇa*, is logically arranged and legendary material is handled with imagination and flourish. The story is told in twenty-eight cantos and touches upon briefly all aspects and major events in the life of the Buddha's life.

In his works Aśvaghoṣa is concerened to draw attention of the *samsāra*-oriented leading characters to the more subtle and sublime path of *nirvāṇa*. The sermons and preaching put in the mouths of his characters and didactic discourses are of gerontological relevance because they deal with subjects such as vanity of the body, impermanence of youth, and the evils of old age. These topics are discussed and elucidated with the help of both simple and elaborate similes and metaphors often inspired by the epics Rāmāyaṇa and Mahābhārata.

Activism, positive engagement, and intervention in worldly affairs underlie Vedic philosophy of life. We have come down, says a Vedic poet, to love and enjoy. Indians of the Vedic age hoped to live a long and healthy life full of vitality. Aging is a natural and a *sui generis* biological process conditioning and circumscribing life. A verse from the Atharvaveda (3:11.8), for instance, states this in a matter-of-fact tone:

> Man is tied down to old age just as a bull is tied down to a post. It is, therefore, futile to fear old age and death and attempt to run away from it.

Another hymn (AV 5:28.7) compares the three stages of human life (youth, middle age and old age) to the three strands of the sacred thread (*yajñopavita*). Just as the same material (cotton) goes in the making of the three strands, in the same manner let *dharma* animate all the three stages of life. The human body is a precious treasure that must be preserved up to ripe old age.

Siddhārtha

According to legends, when Siddhārtha (future Buddha) was born, astrologers predicted that he would either become a world emperor or a renouncer. King Śuddhodana, his father, therefore, took elaborate precautions in order to prevent emergence of renunciating tendencies in Siddhārtha. He was sheltered from encountering any unsavory life experience. On this basic legendary material Aśvaghoṣa skillfully and imaginatively constructs a narrative account of how gods did succeed in fostering in young Siddhārtha renunciative tendencies. As a preacher and missionary Aśvaghoṣa is careful to let us know that the new path that the future Buddha was to take was intended and legitimated by [Hindu] gods themselves.

Exposure to diseases, aging, and death

The gods accomplish their task by acquainting the future Buddha in quick succession with three increasingly unsavory and unpleasant facts and experiences in life: (1) old age; (2) disease, and (3) death (*jarāvyādhimaraṇa*). When Siddhārtha sees an old man doubled up with age, he asks his charioteer (*sūta*), if aging is to be attributed to *vikriya, vikāra, svabhāva, niyati,* or *yadṛcchā.* The charioteer's reply informs us much about the prevalent *brāhmaṇa* understanding of the aging process and the phenomenon of old age. This man says the charioteer, is broken down by old age which robs beauty, destroys the body's strength, is a source of all kinds of sorrow, ends pleasures, wrecks memory and is a foe of all the organs in the body and their functions (*jarānāma yayaiṣa bhagnah* BC 3:30, 36). Know old age to be a *vikāāra*, i.e. modifications brought about in the body and an *avasthāviś śeṣa,* that is, a particular state of the body. The charioteer then adds that the process of aging is a developmental sequence taking place over a determinate period of time. "This man," he adds, "who now is old and bent, first was breast-fed by his mother. He then learned to crawl on the ground and gradually grew into a scrappy lad. The same young man, in due course, has now reached old age."

Siddhārtha is visibly shaken by these words of the charioteer and asks him in trepidation, "Will this evil old age strike me also?" The reply is in affirmative and is further buttressed by the observation that aging is a process which is irreversible, inevitable, unstoppable, universal, and uniform among all men and women (BC 3:32). Echoing the traditional brāhmaṇa views the charioteer then also adds that though cognizant of this fact about old age, people still desire to live as long as possible. Upon hearing these pronouncements on old age Siddhārtha began to tremble like a bull frightened by a lightening. Muttering old age, old age to himself he sauntered away dejected.

When in due course he also learns about the equally ugly facts about disease and death in the similar manner from the charioteer, Siddhārtha decides to retire to the forest to further reflect on the deadly trio old age, disease and death. He cannot understand how sentient beings, in the face of the three evils, can stand, sit or sleep at ease, much less laugh and make merry. They are in fact, he concludes, insentient beings on a level with birds and beasts. It is a great pity that a man who is himself lacking in happiness and who is subject to old age, disease and death should hate another man who, too, is afflicted similarly. Since I share a common human nature with them, I must, reflects Siddhārtha, develop a true insight into the nature of the three evils.

When Siddhārtha questioned his charioteer about the old man, his question was not merely an inquisitive query asking "Who is he," but rather a sympathetic observation, "Why is he so, what has reduced him to this pitiful condition?" Siddhārtha is distressed to find out that the wretched fellow is not only suffering but others old and not so old also despise him. Thus when Aśvaghoṣa states that the scenes of the old man, the sick man and the dead man were not noticed by any except Siddhārtha; it may be understood as conveying that nobody paid particular attention to these conditions of human life. This was a faithful commentary on the typical Vedic attitude about old age at the time.

Promoting renunciation (nivṛtti)

But in Siddhārtha the words of the charioteer produced more intensive desire to renounce the world. He now becomes resolute to go in search of the way to the extinction of burning: the burning of life to death through old age and disease. Prince Udayin, who is of the same age and class of warriors (*ksatriyavarṇa*), is the first to know of Siddhārtha's resolve. Udayin, incidently, was entrusted by King Śuddhodana to shadow Siddhārtha everywhere and keep watch on him. He therefore attempts to dissuade Siddhārtha from renouncing home life, "You Siddhārtha, who are so youthful, strong and handsome, must not despise objects of pleasures (including women) which have justly come to you." To this plea Siddhārtha's answer is, "I do not despise objects of pleasures per se. I am disturbed by their impermanent character. If there be not this trio of decrepitude, disease and death. I, too, would find pleasures in these objects so charming to the mind" (4:86). It is true that in ancient times there have been high souled individuals who desired and made love. But this fact need not lead us to hasty conclusions (i.e. we need not follow their example) because eventually they, too, went to their ruin. Their fate indicates that desire (*kāma*) cannot be an organizing principle of life (4:90). Brooding over the terror unleashed by the evils of old age and disease, I have become very timid and distressed. I find this world as if ablaze with fire. I have no peace, no fortitude. How then can I find pleasure in the objects of love as you suggest? (BC 4:98).

When King Śuddhodana learned about Siddhārtha's firm determination, he too tried, though unsuccessfully, to persuade Siddhārtha. Through Śuddhodana's arguments we learn a great deal about views on life and old age held by Vedic Indians. He went to the forest and performed various rituals prescribed in the Śruti. He hoped that his son would not go to the forest (BC 2:54). His basic argument is that the search for spiritual liberation and peace in the forest is a religious injunction and duty whose time has not come in the case of Siddhārtha. Taking up that task in young age, when the mind is still fickle, is an evil act. The minds of young men, whose senses are preoccupied with objects of pleasures and whose resolve is not strong enough to sustain the tiring austerities naturally shies away from the thoughts of forest life. Young ones simply lack that power of discrimination so essential for a task to be executed in the forest.

Śuddhodana then hastens to remark that as a matter of fact the time was ripe for him, Śuddhodana, to transfer the responsibilities of the kingdom to Siddhārtha and retire to the forest. He concludes his discourse by admonishing Siddhārtha that his true dharma lies in performing heroic deeds. If Siddhārtha were to take to forest life out of turn (*vikrameṇa*), as it were, leaving his aged father the responsibilities if the family, it would be irreligion (*adharma*). Siddhārtha's response to his father's entreaties is curious. He observes that he would delight in winning the pleasures procured by the sense organs provided old age, disease and death did not exist (BC 4:86). There would be no need of *nirvāṇa* had there been no change and transformation in the lives of beings on earth, if they had been eternal, unchanging (BC 24:17):

> I would defer my decision of going to the forest if you were to stand me surety in respect to the following four things: (1) Life should not end in death, (2) disease should not destroy my health, (3) old age should not rob me of my youth, and (4) adversities should not deprive me of my wealth (BC 5:35).

Śuddhodana offers no further comments to the tongue-in-cheek remarks made by Siddhārtha, who soon renounces home in the dead of the night leaving his young wife and infant son; and enters the forest.

When Śuddhodana is informed of Siddhārtha's departure, in sheer desperation, he suggests a compromise: Siddhārtha could reject some of the norms of the householder. He could retire to a room in the outhouse and lead a secluded life within the bounds of the palace taking on select norms of the forest life (in the manner of a *Gṛhamuni)*. Śuddhodana points out that in the past many sages discharged their forest duties without actually leaving the worldly life; precedent thus existed for Siddhārtha to emulate. "Effort and wisdom," concludes Śuddhodana, are the two essential requirements in one's search for peace and spiritual liberation;

not the stay in the forest, which is only an external and outer symbol of renunciation.

But Siddhārtha is in no mood to make compromises. As a last resort King Śuddhodana 's ministers (in their roles as the wise and elderly counsellors) try in vain to remind him of his filial responsibilities:

> In the past heroes such as Bhīşma, Rāma and Paraśurāma listened to their fathers' wishes and acted accordingly. You, too, should act as per the wishes of your father, and gladden his heart. Your young wife Yaśodharā, too, deserves to have you back. Though married and protected, she is now, as if without her lord and protection (*anāthā*, 8:61). You should, therefore, return home to your father and wife (BC 9:27). Further, your decision is not sanctioned by the *śāstras*, nor is it timely (*kāla yukta*). Abandoning your aged father in grief and distress is not dharma but *adharma* (BC 9:53). Young as you are, you are not capable of distinguishing between *dharma* and *adharma*, on the one hand and *mokşa* on the other, which in your case still lies in the distant future. *Mokşa* can only be attained by discharging the three debts incurred by man at birth. One must repay the debt owned to the gods by sacrifice; to the seers by the study of the Veda and to the manes (*pitar*) by procreation (BC 9:65).
>
> In the past those who had entered the forest ahead of time, returned to home life when they realized their mistake. You should, therefore, have no hesitation in returning home (BC 9:71). It is not a sin to revert to the norms of the householder if they were abandoned out of turn (*akāla* = in wrong time).

Siddhārtha remains unmoved by the counsels of the elderly ministers. He essentially repeats the answer he had given to his father:

> I have abandoned my own kith and kin because I am terrified of old age, disease and death *(...vyādhijarā vipadbhyo bhītastvagatya svajanam tyajāmi* (BC 9:31). Time is grabbing everybody at all moments. There is thus no specific period in time when alone a particular task could be successfully accomplished (...*akālo nāsti dharmasya jīvite cancale sati*, BC 6:21).

> I, too, can cite instances of kings in the past who, upon growing averse to the joys of kingdom and comforts retired to the forests. I have made my resolve once for all, and cannot now go back on it (BC 9:38).

Thus burning the bridges behind him, and having entered the forest, Siddhārtha begins the search for a guide who can initiate him to the path of liberation. Thus he chances upon Ārāda , an elderly sage proficient in the doctrines of Sāmkhya and Yoga, and whose wisdom is sharpened and deepened by his advanced age. In the ensuing exchange between the two, we notice that Ārāda , too, reiterates the traditional brāhmaṇa views of the human life cycle:

> It is not unusual to find kings in their old age went to the forest after transferring power to their children. What surprises me, indeed, is to find *you*, you who are still young; you who has not fully enjoyed material wealth and joys of senses, intent on subduing them (BC 12:7, 8).

Siddhārtha's response is predictable. He merely repeats the wish that Ārāda explain to him the path which he may follow to liberate him from the deadly trio disease, decrepitude and death. Ārāda is the last person whose advice is sought by Siddhārtha. But he is not impressed by Ārāda's insights. He therefore sets to find out the path of liberation on his own. When he has made considerable progress in his spiritual quest; Māra, the personification of desire, disturbs the meditating Siddhārtha with this unsought for advice:

> O warrior! Stand up and follow your dharma. Renounce this quest for *mokşa*. Win the world and heaven with arms and proper sacrifices. Born as you are in the famous warrior clan, this path of beggar is unbecoming for you (BC 13:9).

But Māra could not dislodge Siddhārtha from his firm resolve. He was preoccupied with the thought, "In truth, what is it whose very existence is the cause of old age and death?" (BC 14:52) When he finally did emerge from his deep meditations Siddhārtha had become the Buddha (the awakened one). Entering the depths of truth, he had realized that there being birth; old age and death arise (BC 14:53). He then expounds on the causal chain starting with *janma-jarā-maraṇa*. He had found the way of putting an end to old age, disease and death. Soon he was preaching his newfound path to the multitudes in Northeast India.

Saundarananda

Like Buddhacarita, Saundarananda has as its subject matter the theme of conversion: of Nanda, the half-brother of the Buddha. Aśvaghoṣa feels more at home here and pithy dialogues and descriptions of psychological conflicts taking place in Nanda's mind characterize the work. The exposition of the basic teachings of the Buddha (victory of old age, disease, and death by following the eight-fold noble path) by Aśvaghoṣa in Saundarananda is remarkably clear and concise. It wins him the admiration of I-Tsing the devout Chinese pilgrim who visited India centuries later. Two shorter works of Aśvaghoṣa are also significant because they too have the theme of conversion. Sāriputraprakaraṇa, a typical social drama, deals with the conversion of two brāhmaṇa youths to the path of the Buddha. The Rāṣṭrapālanāṭaka is a dramatized version of the story from the Majjhimanikāya, which revolves around the conversion of a rich merchant. The whole process of the conversion of Nanda, the householder, to Nanda, the monk in quest of *nirvāṇa*, may be summarized as follows:

When Siddhārtha renounced the claim to the throne and left home Nanda, his half-brother, became heir-apparent to the throne. Nanda was deeply in love with his young and beautiful wife Sundarī. After Siddhārtha had become Buddha, he paid visit to his parents and the city of his birth. One day he went to Nanda's home for begging food. But the couple was deeply absorbed in love and the Buddha had to leave empty handed. When Nanda learned of this he hurried to the Buddha's quarters promising Sundarī that he would be back soon. But the Buddha had willed otherwise. Nanda wanted to go home out of his love for his wife, but the Buddha confounded him by blocking up the entry of the street. Perceiving that Nanda was intent upon sensual indulgence, he compelled Nanda to follow him. Writhing with grief, Nanda then followed the Guru slowly and helplessly, thinking of his wife (SD 5:14, 15, 19). Nanda was thus initiated into the *samgha* against his wishes. This event sets in motion the transition of the sentiment of love (*sṛangāra*) to that of supreme peace (*śāntarasa*).

Since Sundarī was unaware of Nanda's unexpected initiation, she grows increasingly alarmed when Nanda does not return home. Aśvaghoṣa describes this second stage (*vipralambha śṛngāra*) with consummate skill.

Sundarī wept, she became languid, she howled, she grew exhausted, she paced up and down, she stood still, she wailed, she brooded. She grew angry and threw off her garlands. She scratched her face and tore her garments (SD 6: 34). Then an old woman tried to console her by saying:

> You are the wife of a royal seer and it is not befitting of you to grieve when your lord has taken refuge in law. For the groves of asceticism are the hereditary possessions of the Īkşvāku clan in which your husband was born (SD 6: 39).

But another woman hoped that Nanda will return:

> It may be argued that having taken the mendicant's robe, Nanda cannot now abandon them. But there can be no wrong in leaving it again, when he took it against his will (SD 5: 48).

Nanda, on his part, grows equally restless:

> Bearing with his body but not with his will the insignia of [monkshood] prescribed by the Buddha's ordinance, Nanda grew dejected because his mind kept turning on his wife (SD 7: 1). He laments the difficulties involved in the practice of austerities in the forest while his wife might be weeping at home. Especially who could have such strength of mind in the first flush of youth, in the month of spring, which is said to be the enemy of ascetic life (SD 7: 13). He then goes on to recall instances of mature sages in the past that couldn't resist the charm of women at any age.

Then seeing thus carried away by his youthful vigour and beauty and determined to go home, a monk reproved him saying:

> We both are aware of your strength, beauty and youth. But you do not understand as I do, that these three are ephemeral (SD 9: 4). Where is the strength of Kŗşņa who slew Kamsa? Jarasa struck him with a single arrow, just as old age strikes down, in due course, beauty however great (SD 9. 18). The seasons pass and come around again; the moon wanes and waxes again. But once they have passed away, neither the water of a river, nor the youth of a man returns (SD 9: 28). Do not, therefore, feel pride thinking, "I am beautiful, strong or young. Recognize that

> this great danger of the world known as old age points the way to death (SD 9: 34).

Despite this sermon of the veteran monk, Nanda still remains recalcitrant[40] and the Buddha himself has to intervene. As part of the strategy to induce the sentiment of supreme peace in Nanda, the Buddha brings his half-brother to paradise draws his attention to a one-eyed female monkey. Thereupon Nanda remarks that in comparison his wife Sundarī is far more beautiful. Next the Buddha brings nanda to the harem of Indra filled with extremely beautiful nymphs (*apsarās*). At this nanda is moved to observe, "My wife appears as wretched in comparison with these nymphs as she was superior in beauty to the one-eyed she monkey."

The Buddha then proposes to Nanda that if Nanda were to practice austerities and yoga as instructed by the Buddha, he would win all the heavenly nymphs as his prize. Nanda readily accepts this proposition. Upon returning to earth, Nanda gives himself to austerities etc. with the view of winning his reward. After some time Nanda, who was so fond of his wife, seems even when she was mentioned, to remain free from passion and is subject neither to joy nor to agitation on her account (SD 11:3). Ānanda, the Buddha's chief disciple, on learning that Nanda had settled down, approaches him and remarks:

> It is said that you follow the law (dharma) and practice austerities to obtain nymphs as your prize. You are striving to cultivate self-control for the sake of passion. It is as if a man were to carry about a heavy stone on his shoulder to sit down (SD 11:19).

Ānanda points out the absurdity of Nanda's aim by further admonishing him that:

> As a honey collector overlooks the precipice, so you see the nymphs but not the fall that will ensue at the end. Know, therefore, that love is not true happiness. The quest of love is full of suffering and in its attainment, there is no appeasement of desire (SD 11:29).

[40] Steadfastness in respect of the past, present, and future did not grip his mind in any way because of passion, just as *asti* is said to be used as a particle of all three times (SD 12:10).

Nanda feels highly abashed at being upbraided by Ānanda for giving to the law in order to satiate amorous desires.

> As on seeing nymphs, he had forgotten his wife, so now he gave up the nymphs, in his agitation over the impermanence of his union with them.

Nanda then approaches the Buddha and declares:

> I have no need of the nymphs for the gaining of whom you agreed to stand surety. I release you from that pledge. Having obtained an understanding of the world as it is, I now delight only in the supreme law pronounced by you, the law that destroys all suffering caused by old age, disease and death.

The foregoing indicates how Aśvaghoṣa depicts the transformation of Nanda, the passionate householder into a dispassionate monk. Aesthetically speaking, the initial *śṛangāra* sentiment of Nanda is gradually molded into the sentiment of supreme peace (*śāntarasa*).

In a sermon to Nanda the Buddha further elaborates the basic teachings aready introduced in Buddhacarita. Since the world of the living is blazing with the fires of death, disease, and old age, who would lie down in it without agitation any more than in a burning house (SD 14:30)? Old age, disease, and death are the great dangers of this world; there is no country where these dangers do not exist. Place no trust in this transitory life; for death is ever carrying people off and has no reverence for old age (SD 15:46, 62). Recognize suffering to be birth which is the root of the afflictions, old age etc; for as the earth is the place where all plants grow, so birth is th eplace where all calamities grow (SD 16:7). So long as active beings perish among creatures calamities of many sorts, old age etc. are produced among them; for trees that have not come into existence cannot be shaken, however fearful the winds that blow (SD 16:10).

No reliance can be placed on life for even a single moment. For death, like a tiger lying in wait, strikes down man at any moment. Do not be carried away by the thought that you are strong and young. Death can strike in any age and it does not necessarily respect youth. Place, therefore, no trust in this transitory life.[41] For death is ever carrying people off and has no particular reverence for old age either (SD 15: 53). When thoughts turn to the prosperity or adversity of the family members, investigate the nature of the world of the living in order to cut short the developing attachment to them. It is only delusion that creates the bonds of attachment between persons. He who is your kinsman in this existence, was a stranger to you in the past lives. And in the future, a stranger of today may well become your kinsman.

As travellers come together in a shelter house for the evening, only to part away on their separate ways in the morning; so is one's union with one's kinsfolk (SD 15: 30). A mother cherishes her child only with the thought that he will support her in old age. A boy loves his mother merely because she bore him in the womb. Kinsmen are known to act in unfriendly fashion and strangers friendly. Men and women thus make or break bonds of affection according to their vested interests. As a painter might fall in love with a woman he had himself created (in a painting), so is man attached to man by inventing affection himself. Do not, therefore, let your mind be obsessed with the thoughts of your kith and kin. For, there is no permanent distinction in the cycle of existence between kinsfolk and strangers (SD 15: 36).

Goal of human life

As preached by the Buddha and recorded by Aśvaghoṣa, the goal of human life is emancipation (*nirvāṇa*) from the snares of worldly existence (*samsāra*). The norm of *nirvāṇa* is not unlike *mokṣa*, the fourth goal or end of life (*puruṣārtha*) in the brāhamaṇa tradition. Naturally, the Buddhists could not endorse the first three ends of life. These had to be successfully repudiated. This very enterprise is vigorously pursued by Aśvaghoṣa in Saundarananda. Discarding the puritanical interdiction of Hinayāna on the use of art in religion, he draws on the already popular *kāvya* tradition in composing Saundarananda, which is a highly regarded work of art.

The mundane (*laukika*) ideal of equally pursuing the first three ends of life (*trivargasāmya*) powerfully portrayed in Saundarananda, therefore,

---

[41] But the Buddha does not extend the same logic that he employs in the case of young men to young women. His advice to Āmrapāli, the young and beautiful prostitute, for instance, is that thirst for dharma cannot arise in beautiful and young women (BC 22:41).

pertains to the external aspect of that work. It is no better than a mere hypothesis to be refuted (*pūrvapakṣa*). The transcendental (*lokottara*) ideal of *nirvāṇa*, on the other hand, is a conclusion to be proved (*siddhānta*). It is the principal purpose (*prayojana*) of that work.

It is therefore not surprising that the common thread running through Aśvaghoṣa's works is the conversion of the householder (*rāgin gṛhastha*) to the dispassionate monk (*virāgin bhikṣu*). They portray an ardent and inspired householder in quest of spiritual liberation who fights heroically and ultimately triumphs over the storm of passion and enters *nirvāṇa,* the matchless island of absolute tranquility. In terms of esthetics the passage from the householder to monkshood represents the eclipse of *śṛangārarasa* and emergence of the *śāntarasa*. Following Bhattacarya (1976) it may be said to take place in four stages: The *śṛangārarasa* is first gradually transformed from the condition of depiction and manifestation of carnal joy (*śṛangāra, sambhoga*) to the condition where only one partner may harbour the sentiment of *śṛangāra* (*vipralambha*), to the condition where only the shadow of that sentiment remains (*śṛangāra bhāsa*). Finally, the last tentacles of *śṛangāra* are to be cut by the development of the heroic sentiment (*vīrarasa*) with a view to establish the condition of the sentiment of ultimate peace (*śāntarasa*).

In Saundarananda the stage of *sambhoga* is cultivated through the graphic account of love dalliance of Nanda and his wife Sundarī. The next two stages are presented as the dwindling attachment of Nanda to Sundarī and the nymphs (*apsarās*) in the primary stages of his austerities; and later between the nymphs and the feeling of disgust with respect to desire. The emergence of the sentiment of supreme peace (*śāntarasa*) in Nanda is delineated in great detail by Aśvaghoṣa.

Preaching and conversion activities led by the Buddha and his ardent disciples resulted in a large number of Indians joining the *samgha*. Large scale defections to the *samgha* by the young, married men threatened to create a discord in the harmonious family life of traditional India. An echo of this phenomenon is discernible in Buddhacarita (17:24) which states that upon hearing the Buddha's discourse, a rich and handsome brāhmaṇa youth of Kaśyapa clan abandoned all his wealth and beautiful wife, put on ocher robes, and left home in quest of *nirvāṇa*. On another occasion when the Buddha was visiting his home town, a large number of princes embraced the holy law, rejected Vedic ceremonies, sacrifices, turned their backs to the Vedic endorsement of material pleasures, and abandoned their family members who were reduced to tears (19:38). Others, who were impressed by the Buddha's mastery over various *siddhis*, and his being honored by his father, King Śuddhodana, also wished to live home (19:37).

A Jaina account concerning the Rāṣṭrapālanāṭaka of Aśvaghoṣa states that when this musical play was performed at Kusumapura (modern Patna in Bihar), five hundred noblemen (kṣatriyas) renounced the world. The people of Kusumapura became furious and in order to stop this dangerous trend burned the manuscript of Rāṣṭrapālanāṭaka. But in the long run the asocial Weltanschauung of the Buddha's message could appeal to a relatively insignificant number of youths from the well-to-do families. Occasional forcible conversions (such as Nanda's) were bound to precipitate misconceptions and unfavourable reactions in the contemporary society.

Concluding remarks

Both the Vedic (brāhmaṇa) and Buddhist thinkers concurred that old age entails all kinds of losses in physical and psychological terms. Both more or less accepted that transmigration (*samsāra*) is suffering and that the way out of this predicament is to undergo a spiritual discipline (*sādhana*) involving some aspects of yoga. Where the two traditions did disagree was on the question of just *what* is deemed to be the appropriate time to undertake spiritual liberation. The Buddha argued the best time is *now*. Future is unpredictable, death strikes at any hour. Spiritual discipline is a strenuous enterprise requiring heroic energy and effort which is readily available in plenty in the early years of one's life. The longer the individual remains in the world, the stronger his bonds with his family and community grow, making it almost impossible for him to renounce the world. Network of kin relationships is a product of man's imagination and it only survives because of the vested interests of the people involved.

As against this, the brāhmaṇa view is that old age also brings in its train significant *gains* to the aging individual notwithstanding the heavy losses inflicted by it. What is lost in physical and psychological terms is more than made up in terms of the intellectual and spiritual gains. With increasing age the human mind facilitates the mergence of quiescence which is the substratum (*sthāyībhāva*) for the sentiment of supreme peace (*śāntarasa*). With age the spirit naturally turns inward and becomes retrospective. One disengages from the bonds of attachment to one's family without doing violence to either party.

Though he preached non-violence, the Buddha but did not hesitate to rupture deep, affective bonds with his own father, wife, and the new-born son. Yaśodharā, the Buddha's wife, condemns the new *dharma* of the Buddha which would leave her (his legitimate companion on the road of *dharma*) destitute (BC 8:61). He was willing to sacrifice the stability and social health of his family for his own spiritual welfare. The Buddha's call to youth to renounce their families and join the *samgha* thus was fraught with serious ethical and moral dilemma.

Awareness of this dilemma is clearly discernible in Aśvaghoṣa's writings. He makes the Buddha declare to his own father, King Prasenjit that one must not believe that this path is not intended for the householder. Whether one lives in the forest or at home the eventual winner is one who obtains peace (BC 20:49). Man's standard of measure is his proficiency in yoga, not his age or class origin (BC 20:50). Here, the Buddha seems to recognize that it is not necessary to leave home in search of *nirvāṇa*. He thus contradicts his early insistence on homelessness and vindicates the arguments brought against this option by Yaśodhana, Bimbisāra, Ārāda, and the prime minister. He concedes that some old people inhabiting in the forest are unable to give to the study of yoga and break their vows thereby attain misfortune (*durgati*). On the other hand, those who are householders are able to purify their *karmas* and by remaining diligent attain the highest state (*naiṣṭhikapadam*, BC 20:51). Elsewhere in the same work the Buddha reveals to Yasa, the son of a rich merchant, that there is no prescribed time period in which alone one must attain *nirvāṇa* (BC 16:5). Thanks to the merit of accumulated deeds Yasa was able to attain the ideal of *arhant* in the same body (i.e. as a householder) (BC 16:7).

There is thus tacit admission in Buddhacarita itself that after all a householder, too, can attain *nirvāṇa;* that one's *karma* has a definite role to play in the quest of *nirvāṇa*. It is necessary to have that inner conviction for success (BC 21:11). A householder can participate or share in the life style of the hermit by developing the mental conviction and understanding the doctrine of *anātma* (BC 16:12). For one who has gained proper insight into the nature of *duhkkha*, there is no difference between a householder and the wandering mendicant (BC 16:13). This considerably waters down the initial hard stand taken by the Buddha that *nirvāṇa* can only be obtained in one's youth and in the forest away from the fetters of worldly existence. This is remarkable particularly when one remembers how adamant young Siddhārtha was in rejecting his father's suggestion that *mokṣa* may be obtained by becoming a *vedasamnyāsika,* which was the model already popularized by King Janaka who remained a householder all his life.

Subsequent social history in the Indian tradition suggests that the traditional brāhmaṇa views on old age were eminently practical and pragmatic and, therefore, have prevailed to this day. Later Buddhists tacitly subscribed to the model of life stages (*āśramadharma*). They recognized that attainment of *nirvāṇa* or *mokṣa* is a task that is best left to the final stage in life, i.e. in one's old age.

Chapter 5

Model of successful aging: the case of Dhṛtarāṣṭra [Shrinivas Tilak]

Integrating old age and death into life

In this paper I intend to discuss how to integrate old age and death within life in order to realize the true sense of perfection (*samsiddhi*) of Self and ultimate reality while still living. Another purpose is to examine how the stages of life model proposed in the culture of India positively correlates the process of aging with the increasing urge for self perfection. I will develop my argument with particular reference to the life of Dhṛtarāṣṭra as it is depicted in the Mahābhārata.

Being a veritable encyclopedia dealing with issues of enduring human interests, it is not surprising that the issues of human suffering, old age, and death figure importantly in the Mahābhārata. One comes across dozens of suffering, old, and dying men and women portrayed in ways that reveal the ancient and classical Hindu tradition's cultural, religious, and social attitudes about old age and death that seem in many ways as perceptive as accounts of modern psychology, social gerontology, and thanatology addressing similar issues. This chapter accordingly begins with analysis of the typical Indian perceptions and attitudes toward old age as they come across in the life history of one major character in the Mahābhārata: the blind old King Dhṛtarāṣṭra who learns to make a transition (after some struggle) toward old age and spiritual fulfillment.

It is followed by discussion of how Dhṛtarāṣṭra comes to terms with fate that had previously undermined his capacity for initiative to attain self perfection. In the vastness of the Epic the concept of *karma* and destiny impinge from several different angles: the inevitable progresion of time, the will of this or that god or the curse of this or that sage, results of previous acts. Sometimes fate is used to explain otherwise inexplicable occurrences which even *karma* cannot adequately justify. Often, events unfold as destiny ordains and time (*kāla*) progresses, with individuals enjoying or suffering according to their previous acts. Only at very special instances, will deity like Kṛṣṇa manipulate the course of events. The relevant issue of theodicy is also addressed from the perspective of the Mahābhārata.

Life and career of Dhṛtarāṣṭra: reconciling fate with human initiative

The character of Dhṛtarāṣṭra who figures prominently in the narrative of the Mahābhārata, provides an ideal opportunity to analyze how the doctrine of *karma* (1) creatively mediates between fate or destiny (*daivam*) and human initiative (*puruṣakāra*) and (2) reconciles the partly involontary human nature and character with human will and the desire to be free. It should be stressed at the outset that the dichotomy that is usually posited between fate and human initiative (with fate having an upper hand) in modern studies of Hinduism does not operate in the context of the Mahābhārata. The Gītā explains that the outcome of an event (whether accomplished by the body, speech, or mind) is decided by five factors: material or natural foundation (*pratiṣṭhā*), agent (*kartṛ*), instruments of action (*kāraṇa*), motives (*pṛthak ceṣtā*), and fate (*daivam*) (18:4,5). Fate thereofre is only one of the five factors that jointly determine the outcome of an action. Freely acting agent has as much capability as fate in the shaping of an event or an enterprise that is undertaken. In gerontological terms Dhṛtarāṣṭra's character offers a useful glimpse into how *karma* effectively mediates between the two given ideal stages (or modes) of life: the adult, householder stage with its mission predicated upon engagement with the material and phenomenal world outside and the hermit stage with its mission predicated upon disengagement from worldly affairs toward the world within.

In what follows below the narrative portion of Dhṛtarāṣṭra's character is based on selected episodes from the Ādi, Sabhā, Strī, and Āśramavāsika parvans of the Mahābhārata which deal with issues of Dhṛtarāṣṭra's contest with old age and fate (*diṣṭi*) to which he initially imputes the loss of his sons and the subsequent suffering and increasing conviction that human initiative and self effort can overwhelm fate leading to a sense of fulfilment and prefection (*samsiddhi*). After providing an account of the traditional understanding of the phenomenon of old age and its institutionalization as recommended in the Dharmaśāstras and interspersed with perspectives from social gerontology, I analyze in the light of these two perspectives key events of gerontological significance that take place in the second half of Dhṛtarāṣṭra's life and that enable him to address the issue of fate and destiny with greater clarity. Next follows discussion of the mediating role of karma in the career of Dhṛtarāṣṭra as he learns to negotiate successfully between the forces of destiny and his quest for self-perfection through self-initiative and effort.

Karma and the stages of life model

Aristotle argued that every natural object has a goal or telos, which it is its nature to achieve and the world is an ordered striving for this end and perfection. The Vedic conception of cosmos and society based on *ṛta* is comparable to this Aristotelian view. Telos (inner aim) of one's being is to go home which in the Indian context means striving to exit from the cycle of *samsāra* and attain liberation. Everything in the universe has a telos because everything has a goal, a function, and a purpose. To follow *ṛta* (in subsequent tradition, *dharma*) is, therefore, to maintain the critical order of and in the cosmos and society. This notion of telos comes across in such reflexive expressions in the Veda as "the rivers flow [by the powewr of] *ṛta;*" "the light of the heaven-born morning [has come according to] *ṛta"* the year [is the path of] *ṛta*. That society is ideal whose behavior pattern is homeotelic (to use the expression coined by Edward Goldsmith; from the Greek 'homeo,' meaning the same): righteous behaviour of the constituent members who serve to maintain the critical order. On the contrary, a heterotelic society must be seen as following the way against *ṛta* and dharma, i.e. one that threatens the order of the cosmos and society.

In the Manusmṛti, Manu attempts to reconcile this somewhat static perception of ideal life of harmony and order with common, everyday dynamic human experience of living within time that is passing people by and causing them to age in the process. Manu invested human life with definite meaning using a pattern of symbolism that would be commonly understood by the masses. Though the latter half of life is characterized by declining physical activities, Manu theorized that it is also a period of redefining the aging individual's status in his society as well as initiating the quest for self-realization. Acordingly, he normatively ordered human life in four overlapping stages of twenty-five years duration each. The stages are conceptualized as following one another in a constant and continuous process of cognitive and spiritual growth and fulfillment. They are traditionally identified as the young student (upto age twenty-five; *brahmacārin*), adult householder (*gṛhastha*), aging hermit (*vānaprastha*), and elderly wanderer (*sanyāsin*).

While the main task of the first two stages is development of outward-directed skills of mastering the ego; the final two stages are characterized by the quest for 'inner' spiritual growth and eventual self-realization. The process of aging brings about increased awareness and comprehension of new psycho-spiritual dimensions and emergent symbolic life which was inhibited previously by the preoccupation with the external world. The stages of life theory is predicated upon belief that people are capable of increasing degrees or levels of knowledge as they grow old. This is in agreement with Plato's view that we should underta ke the study of philosophy (by which he means the long struggle to overcome the illusions of life) only after we have reached the age of fifty. Schopenhauer, in turn, also noted that as we age we develop through successive "stages of life," which give one an increasingly accurate understanding of life's meaning (see McKee 1982 preface ix).

The hermit stage is characterized as the ideal time for practicing a variety of austerities (*tapas*) to facilitate such developments. This prescription the aging hermit shares with the young student who is instructed to spend long periods of time in proximity to the fire tending it with fuel and reciting *mantras* in its presence so that the heat of the fire is absorbed and accumulatd within the student. In the Sūtra and the later Śāstra literature the hermit too is invited to 'dry up his frame by the practice of *tapas*.' If he can, he is encouraged to practice a severe form of *tapas* by standing in the midst of the five fires: four fires lighted in the four quarters with the blazing sun overhead (see Kaelber 1989: 116-117). Thus the model of the student stage (*brahmacārin*) served as a prototype to integrate the values and practices of the competing heterodox ascetic orders who practised renunciation. These ascetics were assimilated into the Vedic scheme of life by creating two additional stages of life: hermit and the renouncing wanderer. The hermit is literally one who stays or lives in the forest (*vānaprastha*). The *brahmacārin* similarly spent as many as twelve years of his student life in one of the 'forest academies' that were usually operated and managed by the hermits.

Both the student and the hermit were required to keep their hair and beard and follow a strict regimen concerning food, sex, and sleeping pattern. Both kept the daily recitation of the Veda (*svādhyāya*). The norms and roles of the student which clearly met the approval of the orthodoxy, thus helped prepare for the integration of ascetic's career into the Vedic fold as the herit stage of life. The stages of the student and of the hermit were clearly homologous with the former serving as a form of rehearsal for the latter. The creation of the four-fold order is explained in an episode in the Mahābhārata, where Sage Bhṛgu instructs Bhāradvāja that in days of yore Brahmā himself ordained the four modes of life for the benefit of the world and for promoting righteousness (Śānti 184:8-11). He then describes the duties, roles, and norms that each person occupying a given mode or stage of life ought to perform. Those of the hermit include cultivation of patience and fortitude. He should practice austerities near sacred waters and secluded woods abounding with deer. He should subsist on wild berries and roots. He should spend the day performing various sacrifices and sleep on the ground in the night bearing without regard cold and heat; rain or wind (Śānti 185:1-6).

Aging as career: theory of differential disengagement

One perspective in social gerontology views aging as an inevitable withdrawing process resulting in decreased interaction between the aging person and others in the social system he belongs to. Others may initiate by the individual or the process of disengagement in the situation. His withdrawal may be accompanied from the outset by an increased preoccupation with himself. When the aging process is complete, the equilibrium, which existed in middle life between the individual and his society, has given way to a new equilibrium characterized by a greater distance and an altered type of relationship. The disengagement process focuses on the individual role-complex and the changes that take place in it as the person ages. Disengagement takes place earlier for some than for others due to differences in physiology, temperament, personality traits and life situation. Furthermore, the precise number of bonds broken with the society also depends on the individual's make-up.

As against this view of aging other gerontologists insist that continued, full scale activity; not disengagement, is the proper path leading toward adjustment, high morale, and life satisfaction in one's later years. The activity theory, however, fails to account for significant numbers of old people who do not cope satisfactorily in their later years. This has led some to question that a distinction be made between an individual's role and his role set. Performance of any role (whether instructor, father or a worker) implies a reciprocal relationship between the performing actor and his social milieu. Execution of a role thus rests on the interaction between two or more persons, which then becomes the nucleus of other social relationships and systems.

Disengagement of the elderly, therefore, cannot imply a total withdrawal from all social relations but rather acquisition of a new set of roles. Disengagement thus occurs at different rates and in different amounts for the various roles in an aging individual's role set. Manu's ideal scheme for the hermit reveals a relative measure of concurrence between behavior it recommends for the hermit and the concept of differential disengagement of modern social gerontology. The theory of differential pattern of aging would find support most notably in Plato (*Republic* VII) which represents a middle ground between the activist and the disengagement theories.

The right response to the experience of growing old is neither resignation nor continuation of middle age norms, but the adoption of values and projects different from those appropriate for youth and middle age. Against activism this view affirms that old age means positive discovery of values and meanings different in character from those accessible to us in youth and middle age. Against asceticism it affirms that insights and values achievable in old age are related to worldly needs and interests and are of direct use to the world at large. In contrast to Aristotle's philosophy of disengagement, Plato advocates full participation of the old in governmental power and other positions of social responsibility (McKee 1982: 5).

It is this notion of differential disengagement, I argue, that better explains the traditional ideal of the vānaprastha as well as the transition in the character of Dhṛtarāṣṭra who immediately after the Great War had suffered from recurrent fits of extreme depression and suicidal tendencies. The process of disengagement, in his case, lasts for fifteen years culminating in a state of calm serenity and spiritual fulfillment. The notion of differential disengagement helps us understand the traditional Indian view of aging as an opportunity for discovering one's own inner world as a worthy alternative to the external world with which one has been interacting in the first half of one's life. The tempo of the process of disengagement which can culminate in spiritual maturation and fulfillment quickens with growing age and is demarcated with significant changes and transition in the role complex, value structure, and status identity of the aging individual. This can be demonstrated by analyzing select events that occur in Dhṛtarāṣṭra's later life.

Significant events in Dhṛtarāṣṭra's career

(1) The Mahābhārata narrates the first half of Dhṛtarāṣṭra's life with relative brevity. He was sired by Sage Vyāsa upon Ambikā, the widow of King Vicitravīrya who had died without leaving an heir to the Kuru lineage. But because she had kept her eyes closed during her rendezvous with Vyāsa Dhṛtarāṣṭra, her son, was born blind. His handicap however would be compensated, predicted Vyāsa, by his growing into an illustrious royal sage possessing great learning, intelligence, and energy. He will be equal in strength to ten thousand elephants (Ādi 100.1-10). He is described as *prajñācakṣu* i.e. the one having knowledge as his eye (Ādi 129:5). But he could also be scheming and trecherous when interests of his sons were threatened. He goes along with various schemes of Duryodhana (his eldest son) and Karṇa to get rid of the Pāṇdavas. One involved burning the Pāṇdavas and their mother Kuntī to death; another was designed to sow dissension between the first three Pāṇdavas born to Kuntī and the last two born to Mādrī and promises them that he would not let his half-brother Vidura in on the plot (Ādi chapter 131 ff; 193:4).

Significant clues giving insight into his complex and ambivalent personality and character are provided in the account of the gambling match depicted in the Sabhāparvan. Almost every impoŗtant character that figures in the Mahābhārata is present there either as participant or observer. Dhṛtarāṣṭra emerges as a helpless man of middle age who is torn between two contrary emotions. On the one hand, he aspires to be a virtuous person with the kingly responsibility of upholding dharma; on the other hand, he must protect the material interests of his own and his one hundred sons. But in the final analysis he fails in both these objectives and comes across as a weak and vacillating old man. He yields to the machinations of his brother-in-law Śakuni and the eldest son Duryodhana without much protest. True, he has periodic qualms of conscience, but he gets over them. For instance, he lets free the Pāṇdavas from bondage and restores to them whatever they had lost in the gambling match only after evil omens (such as wailing of a jackal) appear and after Draupadī shames him. But almost immediately he yields to Duryodhana's blackmail and allows the gambling match to take place the second time when the Pāṇdavas once more lose everything and, this time, are forced in exile (Sabhā 63:22,27).

(2) In the Udyogaparvan Dhṛtarāṣṭra figures more prominently as he alternatively tries to satisfy the material interests of his own sons and

those of the Pāṇdavas. He also tries hard to avoid the potential war and destruction which incresingly looms very likely. He particularly has a soft heart for Yudhiṣṭhira, the eldest of the five Pāṇdava brothers (although Yudhiṣṭhira himself reluctantly comes to the conclusion that 'actuated by avarice and seeking his own good Dhṛtarāṣṭra is now behaving untruthfully and unlike a true kṣatriya' (Udyoga 70:8). In numerous episodes Dhṛtarāṣṭra has extended discussions with Sanjaya, his charioteer and trusted counsellor in law, polity, and administration and with Vidura, his half brother and unrivalled ethicist on the proper course of action that he should follow. Vidura tries hard to impress upon Dhṛtarāṣṭra the need of the two Kuru clans to cooperate with each other in order to propser together. He therefore tries to reason with Dhṛtarāṣṭra:

> You brought up the Pāṇdavas like your own sons and taught them everything. They are obedient to your commands. Giving them back their just share of the kingdom, you will be able to enjoy your share with your own sons (Udyoga 33:103-104)
>
> Your son[s] [Duryodhana and his brothers] is as a forest, the Pāṇdavas are the lions of that forest. Without its lions the forest is doomed to destruction, and lions also are doomed to destruction without the forest to shelter them (Udyoga 37:60).

But Dhṛtarāṣṭra remains unmoved by this wise counsel of Vidura. All he does is to reiterate an incoherent comment:

> Man is not the disposer of either his prosperity or adversity. He is like a wooden doll moved by strings. Indeed, the Creator has made man subject to Destiny.

Dhṛtarāṣṭra next engages in a long dialogue with Sage Sanatkumāra on matters of life and death and spiritual liberation (which incidently foreshadows the dialogue between Arjuna and Kṛṣṇa in the Gītā). His initial question is

> I hear that you are of the opinion that there is no Death. Again it is said that the Devas and Asuras practice austerites in order to avoid death. Of these two opinions which is true? (Udyoga 42:2).

Sanatsujāta begins by recognizing that some believe that death can be avoided by particular acts (*karmaṇā*); others deny existence of death altogether. Both of these claims are true. The considered view of the wise is that death results from ignorance.

> I say that ignorance is Death, and the absence of ignorance (i.e. knowledge) is immoṛta lity. It is out of ignorance that the Asuras became subject to defeat and death, and it is from the absence of ignorance that the Devas have attained the nature of *brahman*. God Yama is not death and death does not devour creatures like a tiger. Its form itself is unasceṛta inable. Pursuit of self-knowledge leads to immoṛta lity. That imaginary god (Yama) holds sway in the region of the departed ancestors (*pitṛ*) where those who are swayed by desire and passion end up. To one who has no desire left, death is not terror, like a tiger made of straw (Udyoga 42:3-8, 13).

Dhṛtarāṣṭra is not fully convinced by this line of argument. If knowledge and its liberating power are so effective, he asks, what is the worth of Vedic sacrifices and ritual acts? Sanatkumāra's explanation (anticipating Kṛṣṇa's to Arjuna) is that karma and sacrifices, too, have liberating potential provided one engages in them renouncing desire. A state of inaction, perfect quietude, and the absence of attributes that is generated by such acts is identical to the nature of the Supreme Soul (see Ganguli 1990 4:93-94; fn 2).

(3) Key events that are narrated in the Strīparvan expose the fatalistic bend of Dhṛtarāṣṭra's mind even more poignantly. Here he is portrayed as a neurotic old man given to periodic bouts of depression as a result of the loss of his sons, kingdom, and power. His sorrow is a sorrow of predestination which he curses bitterly:

> I do not recall any sin of mine committed so far in this life the fruits of which I am faced to reap so helplessly.

Assuming that he was about fifty at the time of the dice game; he would be sixty-five when the Great War takes place. In the Strīparvan we also find the explicit references to and an implied link between the process of aging, death, and the intensity of suffering of Dhṛtarāṣṭra caused by the Great War. He is compared to the bare trunk of a tree shorn of all its branches (Strī 1:4). Inconsolable at the loss of his sons, Dhṛtarāṣṭra repeats to Sanjaya he should have listened to Kṛṣṇa, Vyāsa, and Nārada, among others (Strī 1:13). Overcome by grief he blames everything on fate

> My old age, the destruction of all my relatives, and the death of my friends and allies happened because of fate (*daivayogāt*; Strī 1:19).

(4) But Vidura consoles Dhṛtarāṣṭra (as Kṛṣṇa did Arjuna) by pointing out that everything ends in decay; all that comes together or is united eventually falls apart; all life ends in death (Strī 2:3). He emphasizes the inevitability of death symbolized by time (*kāla*). It is not becoming for man, admonishes Vidura, to grieve over that which must happen. He impresses upon the old king the unavoidable and impartial character of death and time:

> No one is agreeable or disagreable to time, best of the Kurus! Time is never an arbiter. Time drags everything away (Strī 2:14).

Vidura then narrates the operative logic of the process of karma: Past karma remains dormant for the one who is sleeping; it stands up for the one who stands, it runs after the one who is running.Whatever auspicious or inauspicious deed we commit we are sure to appropriate its results (Strī 2:22-24). To conclude his advice Vidura narrates a gripping parable that provides yet another clue for understanding our existential situation. A certain brāhmaṇa is lost in a dense jungle where lions, tigers, elephants, and bears roamed freely trumpeting and roaring. It was a dismal scene to frighten even the god of death, Yama. The brāhmaṇa naturally is stricken by terror. In fear he begins to run helter-skelter looking right and left, hoping to find someone who will save him. Suddenly he notices standing in front of him, with open arms, a horrendous looking female. A five-headed snake hisses at him from one side. Reeling away from her in fright, the brāhmaṇa falls in a well covered with grass and intertwining creepers. In sheer desperation he manages to dangle, clutching to a creeper, like a jackfruit ripe for plucking. He hangs there, feet up, head down.

In the bottom of the well he sees a monstrous snake. On the edge of the well is a huge black elephant with six heads and twelve feet hovering. And, buzzing in and out of the clutch of creepers, are giant, repulsive bees surrounding a honeycomb. Honey drips out of the comb and drops fall on the hanging brāhmaṇa. Helpless though he dangles for his life, the brāhmaṇa still relishes the few honey drops. The more the drops fall, the greater his pleasure. But his thirst is not quenched. More! Still more! 'I am alive!' he says, 'I am enjoying life!' Even as he says this, black and white rats are gnawing at the roots of the creeper. Fears encircle him from everywhere: fear of the carnivores, fear of the fierce female, fear of the monstrous snake, fear of the giant elephant, fear of the creeper about to snap, and fear of the buzzing bees. In that flux and flow of fear he dangles, hanging on to hope, craving the honey, and surviving in the jungle of *samsāra* (Strī 5:2-22).

Dhṛtarāṣṭra, however, can grasp neither the moral nor the deper significance of the story. Vidura therefore reveals the key to the story which the wise know is told to motivate the listner to seek escape from wheel of life (*samsāra*): Though literally hanging on to life by a thread and enveloped in multitudinous fears, the brāhmaṇa is yet enchanted by the drops of honey. The jungle is the universe; the dark area around the well is the individual life span. The wild beasts are diseases. The fierce female is decay and decrepitude. The well is the material world. The huge snake at the bottom of the well is Kāla (all-consuming time), the ultimate and unquestioned annihilator. The clutch of the creeper from which the brāhmaṇa dangles is the self-preserving life-instinct found in all creatures. The six-headed elephant trampling the tree at the well's mouth is the year; its six faces are the six seasons; its twelve feet are the twelve months. The rats nibbling at the creeper are day and night gnawing at the life span of all creatures. The bees are desires. The drops of honey are pleasures that come from desires that one indulged in. They are the sap of desire (*rasa* of *kāma*), the juice of the senses in which all drown (Strī 6:4-12).

Vidura's existentialist sounding discourse is just too much to bear for the old blind king and once again he loses consciousness and falls to the ground at the thought of his lost sons. Vidura, Sanjaya, and Vyāsa revive him. But Dhṛtarāṣṭra continues to lament and to blame his fate and destiny again and again for his miseries.

> It is my adverse fate that has caused all my suffering. I do not know how it will end except through the end of my life. I will do just that--right here and now.

When Dhṛtarāṣṭra repeats the talk of ending his life, Vyāsa dissuades him saying all was already fated and Duryodhana was the root cause of the destruction (Strī 8:11-15). Here the Epic uses what Gary Morson, an

American literary theory scholar, has called the techniques of 'backshadowing' and 'foreshadowing after the fact' to treat the past 'as if it had inevitably to lead to the present we know and as if signs of our present should have been visible to our predecessors' (1994: 13, 234). Indologist Alf Hiltebeitel has argued that such a "he should have known better" motif is relevant in Dhṛtarāṣṭra's case because it is precisely the blind king who should have known better. Naturally, Vyāsa and Sanjaya reiterate why he 'should not grieve' for what could not have been otherwise, and the only antidote to his suffering is the 'doctrine of time' (*kālavāda*) propounded by Vyāsa (2001: 58). Vidura and Yudhiṣṭhira thus pull Dhṛtarāṣṭra back from any thought of suicide. Vidura reminds him that life terminated without spiritual realization is without meaning. He urges Dhṛtarāṣṭra to live on and by practicing austerities and yoga attain self-realization. Yudhiṣṭhira, who too, is mourning the tragic loss of his near kin, pleads with Dhṛtarāṣṭra to remain active in the world and accept the role of a foster-father to the surviving members of the Kuru clan. Thus, with the help from Vidura and Yudhiṣṭhira Dhṛtarāṣṭra is able to resolve the dialectic between determinism and free will in favour of the latter, which ultimately generates a positive outcome. Because Dhṛtarāṣṭra successfully overcomes grief and is happy to relinquish his active kingly role for that of the retiring elder counsellor.

(5) Dhṛtarāṣṭra remained the titular head of the joint Kuru clan for fifteen years according to the Āśramavāsikaparvan. It provides comparison between the treatment of old Dhṛtarāṣṭra by Yudhiṣṭhira and Arjuna on the one hand and by Bhīma, Nakula, and Sahadeva on the other. Yudhiṣṭhira, the eldest Pāṇdava, treated the old king far better than his own son Duryodhana. Sheltered in the company of caring Yudhiṣṭhira, Dhṛtarāṣṭra's steadily reducing lifespan causes no personal crisis or loss of morale since he is able to avail himself of two supportive roles appropriate to the process of disengagement: the instructor and custodian of knowledge role to Yudhiṣṭhira and other Pāṇdavas. Having given up the major tasks of the householder, he now relishes the role of the hermit. The controlled reduction of the variety of interactions with society gives him an increased sense of freedom from the norms that previously governed his kingly and familial behavior. The Pāṇdava women on their part made Gāndhārī and Kuntī feel quite at home. Rising early every day, Dhṛtarāṣṭra peformed all required age and class-specific rituals. He made the usual gifts to the brāhmaṇas and had them recite the *mantras* and ofer libations into the sacred fire (Āśrama 3:8-9).

Assuming that he was about sixty-five when the Great War ended, he would be eighty when he decides to become a hermit and enter the stage of vānaprastha. With passing years Dhṛtarāṣṭra realizes that though the process of disengagement is self-perpetuating, it is at the same time, not without obstructions. The mitigated, fatherly role that Dhṛtarāṣṭra tried to project and play is constantly undermined by Bhīma, the second Pāṇdava, who pays him respect only outwardly. Insensitive to the agonizing dependence that old age generates, Bhīma continuously flouts the parental image that Dhṛtarāṣṭra attempts to project. Consequently, low morale and a diminished sense of self-respect mark Dhṛtarāṣṭra's later years. Bhīma never loses an opportunity of taunting old Dhṛtarāṣṭra to such an extent that he could not withstand Bhīma pinpricks (*vāgbāṇa*) after putting up with him for fifteen years (Āśrama 4:12). The choleric and neurotic blind old king grows impatient with Bhīma and in the moments of physical and psychic weakness turns to Yudhiṣṭhira for help. The persistent challenge to the fatherly role he is trying to project unbalances his mind. He concludes that it is now time for his departure from the city to the forest (Āśrama 6:21-23).

(6) Yudhiṣṭhira, however, demurs. But Vyāsa comes to the rescue and finds a solution. Dhṛtarāṣṭra's intended move to the forest, he assures Yudhiṣṭhira, is not prompted by any sense of frustration or ill-feeling towards the Pāṇdavas but because that was the befitting course of action for an aging warrior and kṣatriya. Vyāsa advises Yudhiṣṭhira to formally grant the old king permission to leave because all royal sages in the end must take refuge in the woods (Āśrama 8:1-5). Growing old brings about increased comprehension of new psycho-spiritual dimensions and emerging symbolic life inhibited previously by the preoccupation with the external world. When Vyāsa thus mediates between Yudhiṣṭhira and Dhṛtarāṣṭra over the future plan and course of action for Dhṛtarāṣṭra to follow, he seeks to reconcile the traditional ideal view of the life cycle as expounded by Manu with common, everyday human experience of aging. The transition from the householder to the hermit stage and the concomitant psycho-spiritual changes and developments occur over a period of many years. Turning inward with the help of austerities and various yogic practices gradually replaces the urge to acquire and retain power in the external world.

Necessary preparations, accordingly, are made for Dhṛtarāṣṭra's departure to the forest. Vyāsa seems to exhort his son Dhṛtarāṣṭra to act and act in a particular way with a specific goal in mind. Prima facie,

Vyāsa's advice and Dhṛtarāṣṭra acting on it imply an element of free will on the part of Dhṛtarāṣṭra. But his decision also has input from 'natural' determinism. The aging body is said to determine, facilitate, and support one's spiritual quest (naturally and positively). There is also the factor of cultural determinism in Vyāsa's linking the norm of disengagement with Dhṛtarāṣṭra being a kṣatriya (Āśrama 8:5). Thus, here is an instance of mediation between fate and human initiative with a possibly positive outcome in the future predicated upon a specific course of behaviour.

(7) At this juncture Dhṛtarāṣṭra expresses a desire to instruct Yudhiṣṭhira in the 'science and art of government' to which the latter agrees as a matter of courtesy. The instruction is spread over three long chapters of the Āśramavāsikaparvan covering all areas of public administration, defense, finance etc. Yudhiṣṭhira should appoint, admonishes the old king, only those individuals as ministers who are loyal and trustworthy, clever in the execution of their respective businesses. Qualified brāhmaṇa advisers should counsel them. He should protect the capital with well-secured and guarded citadels etc. He should carefully watch his treasury grow and spend judiciously on what is required for public good (Āśrama chapters 9-12).

(8) When his subjects learn of Dhṛtarāṣṭra's resolve to leave the palace for the woods they assemble in thousands to pay respect to their king. Dhṛtarāṣṭra is visibly moved by their gesture and asks for forgiveness for all the wrongs done to them by him and by Duryodhana. He asks for their formal permission to retire into the forest with his wife. The gathered assembly, too, is overcome with grief and a brāhmaṇa announces on behalf of the asembly that no one individual could be blamed for the Great War and the destruction that followed. All this was fated and destined. In that moment of reconciliation with his subjects the old king utters penetrating insights: He has realized that the worth of the individual is not measured by external trappings or by social rank. It is the self, 'being in itself' in its bare greatness that alone is capable of grasping the heart of reality. This realization is a long way from his earlier fatalistic and suicidal tendency, signals attainent of a higher station on the route to total disengagement (Āśrama 14:1-17).[42]

---

[42] While the existential sense of a loss of meaning to life and the threat of dissolving self is serious, Ricoeur nevertheless points out that in such "nights of personal identity," a certain "apprehension of the self" remains. "But who is *I* when the subject says that it is

Before moving to the forest, Dhṛtarāṣṭra is keen to perform funeral rites for his dead sons even though he is apprehensive of haggling he might have to through with the junior Pāṇdavas over the expenses to be incurred in the performance of the funeral rituals (*śrāddha*). Vidura volunteers to approach the Pāṇdava brothers on behalf of Dhṛtarāṣṭra to ask for adequate cash and other necessary materials. Yudhiṣṭhira and Arjuna gladly agree to his request, but Bhīma strenuously objects to the lavish expenditure. He would rather let Duryodhana and his brothers languish in hell (Āśrama 17:18). But Yudhiṣṭhira overrules him. Next follow extensive giving in charities: from gems and jewels to food and clothing as part of the death rituals. Tellers and scribes made the offering to br_hma_as and other recipients in the name of each departed son as Dhṛtarāṣṭra called out his name. Yudhiṣṭhira spared no expenses to please the king

> Unto him that was to receive a hundred, a thousand was given, and unto him that was to receive a thousand was given ten thousand, at the command of the royal son of Kuntī (Āśrama 20:9).[43]

(9) Accompanied by Gāndhārī and Kuntī Dhṛtarāṣṭra sets upon the journey to the forest. Vidura and Sanjaya escort the party. The Pāṇdava and the Kaurava widows give them a tearful sendoff (Āśrama 24:13). Following the advice of Vidura, they set up a temporary provisional camp on the banks of the river Bhāgirathī. There the party is met by another royal hermit Śatayūpa, a former king of the Kekayas who has retired to the forest after conferring the kingdom upon his son. He takes Dhṛtarāṣṭra to Vyāsa's hermitage where the latter is formally initiated into the stage of hermit. Śatayūpa then instructs Dhṛtarāṣṭra about the intricate rules of forest life. Subsequently, Dhṛtarāṣṭra and his retinue proceed northwards to establish their own *āśrama* on the banks of the river Yamunā where Dhṛtarāṣṭra begins severe austerities. Gāndhārī and others begin their respective *tapas* as prescribed for their age and gender (Āśrama, chapter twenty-five).

---

nothing?" asks Ricoeur. Firmer grasp of the I is possible, he believes, "by balancing it with the promising self" (see Ricoeur 1992: 166-167).

[43] See Ganguli (1990 12: XIV.24).

(10) As vānaprastha, Dhṛtarāṣṭra is paid visits by other hermits in the forest which include the brāhamaṇa sages Nārada, Parvata, and Devala, the royal sage Śatayūpa. Vyāsa, too, drops by for a short visit (Āśrama 26:1-2). Such interaction with other hermits and far removed from the influence of the former reference groups (married, adult men and women in the householder stage) boosts Dhṛtarāṣṭra's morale reaffirming his newly acquired age-specific value-structure. Age-concentrated environment such as the one created in the forest encourages generation and maintenance of the hermit's role as well as distinct age-appropriate normative system recommended by Manu. Since the basis for status acquisition within such adult communities is internally defined, it leads to a sense of community-feeling among fellow-hermits.

Back in Hastināpura, Yudhiṣṭhira and other Pāṇḍavas are anxious to learn about the welfare of the elderly group now voluntarily living in the woods and deprived of their former life of palace luxury. Yudhiṣṭhira decides to pay them a visit and orders preparations for a huge retinue (comprising of all Pāṇḍavas, Draupadī, and all Pāṇḍava and Kaurava widows) that will accompany him to the forest. Upon nearing the forest, everybody alights and proceeds on foot to the retreat. Dhṛtarāṣṭra and his group are very pleased to receive the large party from the capital. Everybody is overjoyed and greetings and memories of olden days are exchanged. The next day Dhṛtarāṣṭra takes Yudhiṣṭhira and his party around the woods to show him the hermitage complex (*āśramamaṇḍala*) and to experience first had the idyllic conditions in which they performed sacrifices and practised austerities.

The thick woods and the greenery were teeming with ascetics and hermits, the smoke of clarified butter slowly curled upwards, herds of deer grazed everywhere, and birds chimed their melodious notes while the peacocks danced. In the background were to be seen large heaps of fruits, nuts, and edible roots. Yudhiṣṭhira then gave away in gift all kinds of material objects of use to the ascetics. Amidst all this, King Dhṛtarāṣṭra blazed with in Vedic splendor like another Bṛhaspati (Āśrama 34:5-20). He inquires from Yudhiṣṭhira about the state of affairs of the kingdom and the subjects. He once again lectures Yudhiṣṭhira on polity and government (Āśrama chapter 33). When Yudhiṣṭhira and other members of the Kuru clan pay Dhṛtarāṣṭra a visit in his hermitage, it boosts his morale because he then is able to revisit and briefly reoccupy the parental role which he had left behind. The opportunity to reoccupy the role of the instructor and once again discourse on the king's duties and responsibilities toward his subjects (*rājadharma*) provides him with an added measure of satisfaction restoring his sense of 'wholeness.'

Before departing Vyāsa asks Dhṛtarāṣṭra what he would like to see or hear (that ordinary motals cannot see or hear) in recognition of the power Dhṛtarāṣṭra had attained by practising austrities (Āśrama 35:24-25). Dhṛtarāṣṭra is unable to decide even after almost a month passes by. When Vyāsa returns, he finds Dhṛtarāṣṭra still brooding. Hearing that Vyāsa, Yudhiṣṭhira and the party is in the forest, Nārada, Śatayūpa and others once again join Dhṛtarāṣṭra and his guests from the city to listen to Vyāsa's discourse (Āśrama 36:7-9). Vyāsa finally declares he knows what is troubling Dhṛtarāṣṭra, Gāndhārī, Kuntī, as well as Pāṇdava the Kaurava widows: they are all grieving after their loved ones. Vyāsa therefore resolves to show them the Kaurava and Pāṇdava sons and husbands who were slain in the Great War. Later, he instructs all to proceed to the banks of Gangā. There through Vyāsa's great ascetic powers (*tapas*), everybody sees with great joy the vast army of the dead heroes reappear in the bed of the river. Dhṛtarāṣṭra, too, sees them with his 'divine eye' (Āśrama 40:20-21). Vyāsa then offers the widows the opportunity to rejoin their departed husbands. They all accept his offer without any hesitation and plunge into the waters (Āśrama 41:17-21). Through this favour of Vyāsa the surviving members (old and young) of the Kuru clan are able to dispose of their grief for the departed loved ones.[44]

Narration of this event also provides the Epic an opportunity to insert an explanatory note on its view of the acting out of one's karma. When King Janamejaya learns of the dead Kuru heroes reappearing in flesh and blood before their surviving kins in the river bed, he asks Sage Vaiśampāyana,"How is it possible for persons whose bodies have been destroyed to reappear in those very forms?" Vaiśampāyana's explanation is that acts are never destroyed until agents have enjoyed their consequences and/or endured by patients. Each individual's physical body with identifying features marks etc results from consequences of particular acts. The five cardinal elements coexist with the Lord of the universe and of all beings (Karmādhyakṣa?). They are not destroyed when

[44] Alf Hiltebeitel points out that the Kaurava widows' grief for their husbands is a surplus that is disposed of by Vyāsa. Belvalkar opines that, "The problem of the future of these poor and helpless ladies had hence to be faced and settled. Fortunately, with Vyāsa's special favour most of these were united with their dead relatives" (Hiltebeitel 2001: 82, 83 fn 174).

the material bodies are dispersed and resolved back into the five elements. Only acts that are done without 'exertion' (i.e. in the spirit of disengagement = *nivṛtti*) are true and bear the real fruit of spiritual liberation (Āśrama 42:6).[45] As long as one's acts are not exhaused (by enjoyment or endurance of their fruits good or bad), so long does the ordinary individual regard the body to be one' self. The one of wisdom whose acts have been exhaused does not take his/her body to be the self. Such a person is freed from the obligation of the body (Āśrama 42:1-9; Ganguli 1990 12:52-53). By doing a meritorious act in one's human form and frame, one will enjoy its good consequences in one's human body. The acts peformed mentally affect the mind and those done with the body affect the body (Āśrama 42:17; Ganguli 1990 12:54, fn 1).

(11) Vyāsa then advises Dhṛtarāṣṭra to formally grant visiting Yudhiṣṭhira, the other Pāṇdavas, and Draupadī the permission to return to the capital of Hastinapura which he does only reluctantly as does the party--reluctantly. Two years pass by when Nārada comes to visit Yudhiṣṭhira in Hastināpura. When asked by the latter about the news of his hermit mother Kuntī, Dhṛtarāṣṭra and Gāndhārī, Nārada narrates to him how all three had voluntarily invited death. Soon after Yudhiṣṭhira's return to the capital, goes on Nārada, Dhṛtarāṣṭra began fierce austerities indicating his conviction that he had completed the vānaprastha stage and that now was the time to enter the next stage of life: the wandering ascetic (*sanyāsa*) involving total disengagement from the world. Gāndhārī and Kuntī support Dhṛtarāṣṭra in this decision and the trio began wandering in the woods as renouncers. Within six months Dhṛtarāṣṭra was reduced to mere skeleton. Gāndhārī subsisted on water alone and Kuntī ate only once a month (Āśrama 45:12-14). One day while Dhṛtarāṣṭra was bathing, Sanjaya (who was attending on him and stood nearby) noticed the part of the forest at a distance where Gāndhārī and Kuntī were standing suddenly catch fire. Sanjaya urged them and Dhṛtarāṣṭra to hurry and move away from the path of the fire. But Dhṛtarāṣṭra ordered Sanjaya to leave the forest while advancing himself in the direction of the two women saying

> This death cannot be calamitous to us, for we have left our home of our own accord. Water, fire, wind, and abstention

---

[45] Nīlakaṇṭha, one of the commentators of the Mahābhārata, explains that acts performed with material joys and goals in mind imply mind that is implicated in *samsāra* (*pravṛttidharma).* The soul of such persons becomes embodied and enjoys and endures consequences of his acts (see Ganguli 1990 12:53 fn 1).

from food, (as means of death), are laudable for ascetics (Ganguli 1990 12:59).

From the distance, Nārada continues, Sanjaya witnessed the trio sit facing the east and calmly greet the leaping flames of fire and perish in it (Āśrama 45:29,31).

Discussion

The character of Dhṛtarāṣṭra (as portrayed in the Epic) wavers between two opposite options--surrender to fate or perform assigned age-specific tasks to attain perfection. The main narrative action involving Dhṛtarāṣṭra is interrupted with all kinds of didactic and performative tales (or more precisely perloctionary acts) adding the vector of past and precedent to present and future of his character; summarizing his particular life history as he veers toward one of the options. They index his actions and options inscribing his relationships with other major Epic characters: particularly, Duryodhana, Yudhiṣṭhira, Vidura, and Vyāsa. Dhṛtarāṣṭra serves as a point of intersection for multiple relationships. He is called upon to adjudicate in the dice game twice: almost as if rehearsing it once and playing it for real a second time. A. K. Ramanujan compares such action to a neurotic compulsion to repeat ceṛta in 'autonomous complexes.' It is as if there is a kind of autonomy of action. Once set into motion, the act chooses its personae and constitutes its agents (Ramanujan 1991: 437-440).

An interesting feature of the vānaprastha stage as exemplified by Dhṛtarāṣṭra is the opportunity provided for the older person to join with others of his/her age group in a common cause and activity. Frequent and continued interaction with each other removed from the influence of the reference group of householders seems to foster group solidarity among the elderly. Age concentrated environment in the forest provides an ideal setting to promote relevant and appropriate norms and roles for the elderly. This is corroborated by social gerontology which records positive correlation between residence in age-concentrated setting and higher level of morale and life satisfaction which facilitates self perfection.

The rationale behind the stages of life model can be explained in terms of Ricoeur's notion of 'practices,' which posits different units of praxis that an expanded theory of action ought to encompass (Ricoeur 1992). As the basic unit, 'practices' comprise of the network of subordinate actions governed by constitutive rules that are operative in a particular field: a stage of life, gender, professions, art, and games. Ricoeur calls them 'nesting relations' because they are not linear but belong to the complex of subordinate actions. These actions gain meaning only by the notion of constitutive rules where a given action has meaning and effect only in a particular context [the stage of life, class, or gender]. Thus the role and the norms prescribed for the aging hermit are nested within the stage of the student. Both have 'practice' of austerities (*tapas*) as the defining and mediative value and norm.

Another explanation that may be offered to account for the positive correlation between an age group and specific norms is that a greater amount of contact occurs among the elderly in age-homogeneous environment, which tends to encourage generation or maintenance of roles and a diṣti nctive, age-appropriate normative system. In the process prior occupational and class status or affliation is likely to lose significance. Basis for status within such adult communities tend to be internally defined. A sense of egalitarianism is often the result, which is consciously encouraged. Thus there is no overt reference to the class (*varṇa*) status of the hermit. Again, ascetic practice seems to be the crucial mediating factor that brings hermits belonging to different classes in common cause and goal in the forest (Vyāsa, Śatayūpa, and Nārada belong to different *varṇas* but they can come together as hermits in a common pursuit).[46]

Activity norms in such age-homogeneous environments tend to be defined in terms which are more appropriate for older persons. Although in the Epic cultural context they appear far more strenuous than norms held by any community at large. Our analysis of Dhṛtarāṣṭra's character suggests that the Mahābhārata presents old age as a valued status with ceṛta in privileges not available to younger adults. But old age in itself is not viewed as necessarily worthy of honor (as Bhīma's behavior toward Dhṛtarāṣṭra indicates). The esteem in which the aged are to be regarded is expressed in tangible form in encoded pattern of social institutions and

[46] Occasionally, one also comes across independent female hermits like Śāndilī who practised austerities in the forest (see Śalya 53:6-8). There were women heads of such āśramas like Srucāvatī, daughter of Sage Bharadvāja. She was a female celibate (*brahamcāriṇī*) who had taken the vow of performing severe austerities in order to win Indra, King of Gods, as her husband (Śalya 49:1-2, 13-14).

myths. The elderly in turn are depicted as repository of traditional lore and knowledge, which they transmit to successive generations.[47]

It is significant that Dhṛtarāṣṭra himself decides the number of bonds he will break and the extent to which he will relinquish the role of the head of the Kuru clan. He also invites Gāndhārī and Kuntī to proceed with him to the forest, which they gladly accept and do. He wishes to retain select elements of his status as the householder and accordingly substitutes for his former kingly and authority figure the role of the instructor. Thus he does not totally abandon his career-enhancing central role; neither does he abandon completely the power component from his social status.[48] Furthermore, he has strengthened the prerogatives of the fatherly and instructor role--or at least so he thinks. The roles Dhṛtarāṣṭra acquires and then progressively renounces are: (1) foster father, (2) instructor, and (3) hermit undergoing austerities. These role changes are accompanied by concomitant changes in his value and status structure. In implementing this strategy of diferential disengagement, Dhṛtarāṣṭra is helped by members of his close family and friends (particularly, Gāndhārī, Yudhiṣṭhira, and Sanjaya) and peers and friends like Śatayūpa. His disengagement process however is not quite smooth. Bhīma continuously foils his attempts to fulfill the role of the foster-father.[49]

---

[47] Dhṛtarāṣṭra's status and life style in old age seems to corroborate with the observation of Irwin Pres and Mike McKool that the four prestige-generating components that are operative in all societies: (1) Advisory: degree to which the advice and opinions of aged are heeded; (2) Contributory: degree to which aged participate in and contribute to ritual and economic activities; (3) Control: degree of direct authority the aged have over the behavior of other individuals, institutions or ritual processes; and (4) Residual: degree to which the aged retain prestige due to entitlement resulting from roles performed earlier in life (Press and McKool 1972).

[48] Vyāsa's view compares favourably with modern social gerontology. Viewing aging as a career provides an alternative to the usual conception that growing old is simply a series of losses to be endured. On the contrary, it introduces the idea that although "losses do occur with the passing of years, gains are clearly accrued as well. However, these gains are not equally distributed to all, and the analogy to a career in its everyday sense of the meaning also suggests the idea of differential success. In every society the rewards possible in old age depend to a great extent on the individual ability, resourcefulness, good judgment, and luck during the life cycle" (see Breytspraak 1984: 100-101).

[49] Dhṛtarāṣṭra's role-exit may be better understood in light of the relevant discussion of Helen Ebaugh (1988). She defines role-exit as the "process of disengagement from a role that is central to one`s self-identity and the reestablishment of an identity in a new

On the other hand, there are noticeable positive features: movement away from fatalistic, suicidal tendencies toward a calmer and more serene spiritual maturation. While immediately after the Great War he is repeatedly brought down by inconsolable grief and bouts of depression attributable to the fatalistic tendencies of character, timely advice and counsel given by Vyāsa, Vidura, and Sanjaya enables him to work out his own ego integration toward the end of his life. As Linda Breytspraak observes in this context, the losses of the later years have the potential for releasing new creative developments in the person's selfhood. All transitions and passages require a "mourning-followed-by-liberation process" in which one mourns and comes to terms with the parts of the self that can no longer be, the lost others, and the unfulfilled hopes and aspirations, and then is released to face reality as it is and can be. The focus, therefore, cannot be on resignation and adjustment to losses alone; but also on helping the individual amplify strengths that may be specific to later life (Breytspraak 1984: 45).[50]

Dhṛtarāṣṭra's suffering underscores the classical Indian understanding of the doctrine of karma with reference to old age and aging. To the question what caused his pain and suffering, the Epic provides four possible answers: (1) the sinful deeds of his own eldest son Duryodhana [initiative of an agent]; (2) the will of God [suffered by Dhṛtarāṣṭra, the patient]; (3) the death of his sons and the resulting suffering was destined at a ceṛta in time (as Vyāsa explains); and (4) result of Dhṛtarāṣṭra's own deeds imputable to his greed, cupidity, and *hubris*. These different answers do

---

role that takes into account one's ex-role." What is the meaning of the role-exit process to those who undertake it? Ebaugh proposes the following stages: (1) the aging individual begins to question the role commitment previosly taken for granted, due to such factors as fatigue or disappointments and changes in relationships; (2) seeking and weighing age-specific role alternatives which involves conscious cuing, anticipatory socialization, role rehearsal, and shifting reference groups; (3) the turning point; and (4) establishing a new identity (Ebaugh 1988).

[50] Dhṛtarāṣṭra's character as it drawn by Vyāsa suggests that old persons are not fearful of or preoccupied with death. Rather, death becomes incorporated as an aspect of the selfhood. As Marshall puts it

> (T)he realization of finitude intimately binds together self and death. The self becomes self-as-dying. The hyphenations that link the three terms create a new reality for the individual...Making sense of self is seen as preparatory for the good death (Marshall 1980: 107).

not necessarily contradict, except possibly the first with the remaining three. The Great War is the instrument of death and suffering which must come at appointed time. Destiny, however, is not a blind force because suffering of Dhṛtarāṣṭra is shaped, in part, by his own deeds. This is the prevailing doctrine of destiny in the Mahābhārata. On the other hand, Vidura who views Dhṛtarāṣṭra's sinking into determinism and fatalism as abetting evil categorically contradicts it. This critique of absolute fatalism indicates the major tension in the epic on the subject of destiny, which is eloquently played out through the life of Dhṛtarāṣṭra. His character frequently ascribes calamities to destiny. Upon learning from Sanjaya that the soldiers of the armies of the Pāṇdavas and Kauravas had been arrayed on the battlefield of Kurukṣetra, Dhṛtarāṣṭra reverts back to the fatalistic mood. "I find destiny to be supreme and [against it] human initiative to be a disaster."Although I am fully aware of the outcome of the imminent war, he says to Sanjaya, "I am unable to restrain my son...that will be which must be" (*...yadbhāvi tatbhaviṣyati* (Udyoga 156:7(a). One suspects that he is thereby trying to obscure his own culpability and avoid imputability by blaming his fate.

Sanjaya tries to pull Dhṛtarāṣṭra up from his self-pitying moralizing. Man [or woman] is never the real agent of his/her acts whether right or wrong. Lacking freedom of willed action, he/she is made to act like a wooden contraption mounted on a machine. Sanjaya three possible forces controlling the human agency: the will of deity, result of one's past acts, or consequence of free will). Thus the individual is pulled like a plough in threefold manner (Udyoga 156:14-15). The use of the stock phrase involving the formula '*kecid...kecid...anye*' in this verse reveals a useful hermeneutic strategy of introducing a variety of competing perspectives on a given issue for debate. Typically, the debate ends without resolution. It is important to note that dominant orthodoxy is not allowed to impose a true or correct creed on behal of either destiny or free will.[51]

Our study of Dhṛtarāṣṭra's character and life history reveals the central structuring principle of the Mahābhārata: repetitive action nested in

---

[51]British theologian Nicholas Sutton observes that in the Mahābhārata the role of both destiny (*daivam*) and exertion (*puruṣārtha*) are recognized so also the tension between them which must have been a feature of the debates of the period in which the Epic was formulated. Just as different religious tendencies are accpeted to meet the spiritual needs of different personality types, so either destiny or exertion may be stressed as is deemed most appropriate (Sutton 2000: 384).

interacting structures of repetition, elaboration, and variation. Events in his life are enmeshed in repetitive phrases, similes, and formulaic descriptions. His relentless march toward old age and death is accompanied by the suggestion of regress in motivation. Yet, what is presented in "close-up" (in the last three years of his life) and in dramatic terms is the present life. His character knows what he is doing or did and yet still does it. Vidura and Sanjaya forewarn Dhṛtarāṣṭra against allowing Duryodhana and Śakuni dupe the Pāṇdavas in the dice game. But he still lets them cheat--twice! His actions do not go unrecorded or unreported. They do not remain unjudged or unexpiated. This follows the general belief that no action (whether in mind, body or speech) can pass unpurged or fade without expression and consequence in the world outside the self. Once it begins in thought or feeling, no action can be repressed. When he is grieving on the battlefield over the loss of his sons, the Pāṇdavas approach Dhṛtarāṣṭra to comiserate. He reluctantly embraces Yudhiṣṭhira and then seething inside in uncontrollable rage he asks for Bhīma (Strī 11:12-14). When the latter unsuspectingly moves forward, Kṛṣṇa pulls him back and pushes an iron statue into the blind old king's embrace. Dhṛtarāṣṭra (who is said to possess the strength of ten thousand elephants) easily crushes the effigy into pieces in a tremendous upsurge of repressed anger. Released of that expressive vengence Dhṛtarāṣṭra falls to the ground vomiting blood. Purged of his grief and rage, he is now sorry for what he believes to be the evil act of murdering Bhīma (Strī 11:15-19). Kṛṣṇa then consoles him explaining that he had only pulverized an iron statue and chides Dhṛtarāṣṭra for enteṛta ining such a murderous intention. Bhīma was only an instrumental cause of his grief which was really of his own making. He concludes the sermmon by advising Dhṛtarāṣṭra to read the Veda and other scriptures and to atone himself suitably (Strī 12:1-2). In the end his character indeed undergoes radical change--one of knowledge, a shift from ignorance to liberating knowledge.

Dhṛtarāṣṭra's constant repartees with Bhīma reveal the inadequacies of ordinary morality or the hubris of practical wisdom. His character presents unanlyzable mixture of constraints of fate and deliberate choices as well as the purgative effect of the spectacle itself at the centre of the passions it produces. And yet Dhṛtarāṣṭra's tragic life story is also educative for the reader because it brings out something unique about the unavoidable nature of conflict in moral life. His life touches the agonistic ground of human experience where we witness the interminable confrontation of good and evil, old age and youth, and society and the hermit. The moral lesson that his tragic life and death has to convey to the reader is that the conflicts depicted in the Epic are intractable and not subject to facile resolution. We notice a gap between the practical wisdom taught in the Gītā and the tragic wisdom expressed by the character of Dhṛtarāṣṭra. We are also forced to recognize the gap between the sense of responsibility generated by its relation to fragility and the more traditional sense of responsibility imputed for being the author of this or that act. This latter is turned toward the past. We assume responsibility for repairing the damage caused by our actions in the past or we assume the penal consequences of punishable actions. Thus it is always towards *retrospection* that we are drawn. Bhīma and the younger Pāṇdavas assume responsibility to Dhṛtarāṣṭra's welfare in this sense. But the appeal to responsibility that Yudhiṣṭhira sees [with Arjuna] as coming from fragility of Dhṛtarāṣṭra differs significantly from that of his younger brothers. The concern for him is: what must we do for this fragile being? We are directed towards the future of his being in need of help to survive and to grow. The appeal, the injunction, and the trust that proceed from the fragile result in its being *another* like Dhṛtarāṣṭra who declares us responsible, or as Levinas says, calls us to responsibility. Another, by relying on me, renders me accountable for my acts (Ricoeur 1996: 17).

Dhṛtarāṣṭra's relationship with Yudhiṣṭhira, on the one hand, and with Śatayūpa and other fellow hermits on the other hand, brings out the social and psychological nuances imbedded in the act of initiative and receptivity respectively. The moral command that designates Yudhiṣṭhira as its recipient enjoins him to take the initiative. The 'suffering' of Dhṛtarāṣṭra, which precipitates Yudhiṣṭhira's initiative and compassion, gives him the satisfaction of becoming a benefactor. Inversely, Dhṛtarāṣṭra the sufferer, teaches the benefactor a lesson inasmuch as he extracts from Yudhiṣṭhira (as in Greek tragedy) the confession of sufferer's (and his own) frailness and mortality. The relation of friendship with Śatayūpa and other hermits wherein Dhṛtarāṣṭra associates with on terms of equality, in contrast, appears as a 'mean' between extremes of initiative and receptivity. Following Ricoeur it may be argued that in the character of Dhṛtarāṣṭra, the Epic makes a voice heard which is other than the voice of either *daiva* or dharma as implied by Manu or Yājñavalkya. It is a voice that transcends both: it is the voice of tragedy.

Chapter 6

Vānaprasthāśrama as a vrata [S. Kalyanaraman]

Righteous living by the stages of life model (āśramadharma) is a social ordering for transcendent (*adhyātmika*) pursuits, governed by the goals of life (*puruṣārthas*) which constitute the foundation for impelling everyday actions (*vratas*) based on the triad (*trivarga*) of *dharma* etc providing guidelines for righteous action in life. Conduct appropriate to an office or acquisition of wealth to be shared in a commonwealth and enjoyment of the phenomena are actions natural to many living species (*jātis*). Hence, Patañjali in his Yogasūtra (2.31) notes in a profound sūtra (thread of wisdom):

> *Jāti deśa kāla samaya anavicchinnah sarvabhaumah tad mahāvratam*
> Mahāvrata is [performed in] universal, unbroken, unpartitioned living space and regions, time, and particular moments.

This can also be explained as the core of yoga, the ceaseless quest for uniting self (*ātman*) with supreme self (*paramātman*), this is the great vow (*mahāvrata*).

Vrata

The term, '*vrata*' occurs in the Ṛgveda about 220 times connoting (1) deeds or functions of divinities and (2) divine ordinances about conduct or vows to be fulfilled, in community living. Semantically, it gets elaborated in Samskṛta tradition as steadfast determination and disciplined living.

Indra, the praised of many, associated with Ṛbhu, and with Vaja, exults with Śaci, at this our sacrifice; these self-revolving (days) are devoted to you, as well as the ceremonies (addressed) to the gods, and the virtuous acts of man. [Śaci = karman, act, rite](Ṛg 3:60.6)

Discerning and sagacious, Mitra and Varuṇa, by your office you protect pious rites, through the power of the emitter of showers; you illumine the whole world with water; you sustain the sun, the adorable chariot in the sky (Ṛg 5:63.7)

Vrata in relation to āśrama

Vrata and the four stages or orders of life are correlated. After fulfilling one's responsibilities (*vrata*) during the earlier stages of life (*brahmacarya* and *gṛhastha*) the vānaprastha enters the arena of *vrata* of deeper introspection in order to re-live the stage of *brahmacarya* on the plane of personal consciousness of internalized life-experiences (*anubhūti*). The triad of *śruti-tantrayukti-anubhūti* is a methodological framework for acquiring knowledge which is transported to the plane of knowledge *(jāna)* combined with compassion.

Jñāna is a treasure passed on to the next generation, the generation which is governed by *ṛṇa* (debt) a living principle that puts into practice remembrance of the debt owed to one's departed ancestors (*pitṛs*), gurus and deities who provide one with identity. They make us what we are and act as role models for making our lives a fruitful (artha), an enjoyable experience rooted in *dharma* and *artha*. These are perceived by sages (*mantradraṣṭā*) as eternal and universal (*sanātana*) what Gautama, the Buddha, referred to as '*esa dhammo sanatano.*'

Vānaprasthāśrama

It is a realization of the responsibility owed to the community (*samāja*) at large. What was a personal experience of the two earlier stages of life evolving the full potential of one's proclivities, capabilities and preferences, is now put into action at the level of service (*sevā*) of society. The inner consciousness then merges with the external consciousness in that act of *mahāvrata* fulfilling the quest for achieving unity of *ātman* with *paramātman*.

vānaprastha is not retirement, though for some this may be a prelude to *sanyāsa*, total renunciation of worldly riches and desires. *Sanyāsa*, however, is NOT retirement; rather, it is active involvement by reaching out to the community by sharing the attained *anubhūti*. Our lives become meaningful only by rendering service (*sevā*) to the community. This meaningful fulfillment of the goal of life is specific to vānaprasthāśrama. It is addressed in the Gītā by Kṛṣṇa:

Karmaṇyevādhikārahste mā phaleṣu kadācana

Your right and obligation is to perform your assigned duty; never aspiring for the fruits of your duties. This level and degree of active detachment is referred to as the particular task of vānaprastha in the traditions evolved in Hindu civilization. Institution of such social ordering (governed by *dharma* and *vrata* which are both inviolate) in modern times can provide a framework for a New Global Order.

Vrata in relation to dharma

Vrata, like *dharma*, is inviolate and cannot be broken by gods (devas) or antigods (asura) (Ṛg 5:72.2).

> Steady are you (Mitra and Varuṇa) in your functions, whom men animate by (their) devotion; come and sit down upon the sacred grass to drink the Soma libation (Ṛg 5.72.02).

Manu, too, elucidates the importance of *vrata* in the context of discussing a king's duties:

> Just as the mother earth gives equal support to all the living beings, a king should give support to all without any discrimination (9: 31).

The centrality of *yajña* and *vrata,* thus, is the dominant phase in the evolution of the tenets of Dharma. This phase also absorbed thoughts related to two other fundamental precepts: *ṛta* and *ṛṇa*. The locus of Dharma is delineated in the cosmic context (*ṛta*) and the focus of continuity in tradition is exemplified by the social memory of the debt (*ṛṇa*) owed to the *pitṛs* (departed ancestors) and the repayment of debt owed to society by every individual as a social being.

The precepts of *ṛta* and *ṛṇa* are also fundamental to the next phase in the evolution of philosophical speculations and thought recorded in the Āraṇyakas and Upaniṣads, in the continuum of the Vedic corpus of texts. Philosophical thought expands into a doctrine of transmigration of souls and it is complemented by the endorsement of the practice of asceticism. By 6th to 4th centuries BCE, it also receives endorsement from the Buddha, Mahāvīra, the Jina and Ājīvikas. The heterodox forms of asceticism are thus a continuum, derived from the early orthodox forms of asceticism exemplified by the persons sitting in yogic postures on epigraphs of Sarasvati Civilization[52].

[52] This brief note is based on *Sarasvati: Epigraphs* by S. Kalyanraman (2003 The monograph in reference to the vratya tradition, draws from the references cited in: V.W. Karambelkar, 1969, Vedic Mahavrata, in: *KR Cama Oriental Institute Golden Jubilee Volume*, Bombay, pp. 159 to 178; Radhakrishna Choudhary, 1964, *The Vratyas in Ancient India*, Varanasi, The Chowkhambba Sanskrit Series Office; Chowkhamba Sanskrit tudies,Vol. XXXVIII; and J. Hauer, 1927, Der Vratya, Stuttgart).

Chapter 7

Vānaprastha in the Western context [Greesh C. Sharma]

Introduction

All human societies have life planned out in phases or stages applicable to their geo-cultural context. They prescribe patterned responses to their existential problems as well as to bring order and uniformity. Some cultures are more humane and global in their thinking than others. While others seek solutions by dominance and control of others instead of self-examination and personal growth; more spiritually advanced societies go beyond dealing with existential dilemmas, prescribing means and methods for personal and community transformation and transcendence. Remarkably, societies from Amazon tribes to that of modern nations evolve life-phase planning seemingly guided by cosmic destiny or collective unconscious.

From birth to death, we prepare for different things: some for material gains and others for pleasure and endeavors contrary to realization of spirituality or Moksha. Many within our societies do not bother to plan at all and just live day by day, letting life's events sway them whichever way the wind may blow. Particular individuals, families and societies living in crises, colonialism, terrorism, slavery, civil war or extreme deprivation typically experience a loss of trust in the future and in the ability to sustain any sense of control over destiny. Thus destiny, indeed, cannot be controlled nor created in the absence of safety and freedom.

Living never stops nor does it prevent the arrival of the future. The business of existence goes on for the tiniest of the insect to the most powerful human being in a manner as if determined by fate. However, regardless of one's mental state or circumstances, having a blue print for life is a more productive strategy than having none. We have a source and point of origin and inevitably a destination. It is wiser to put some consciousness and energy in working out one's journey. Of course, the path, the manner, the medium will differ based upon the time, place and context of one's existence.

Blueprints for living do not have to be concrete, rigid and paralyzing. In the western cultures, children are expected to acquire adequate skills to become independent, to manage feelings and meet the challenges of adult life. It is a preparatory phase, but due unfortunately to an overemphasis on independence, the message communicated to youngsters is to grow up really fast and engage in adult like activities as soon as possible. In the USA, for example, sexual activities, drinking, driving and other negative adult pursuits based on rebellion and need to rehearse are markers of the passage to adulthood.

Four Ashramas in Hindu Dharma

There exists another alternative, Four Ashramas in Hindu Dharma. These are the prescriptions for each order/phase of life from birth till the age of 100. The rational behind these four ashramas are to ensure Somato-psycho-socio-spiritual harmony within and with the world and the growth of the body-mind in the most positive way through natural cycle. In Hindu culture the childhood is considered from birth till age 12. The body matures in an evolutionary manner and it should not be force-fed or over stimulated. Hindus adhere to providing the child structure, boundaries, modeling and affection. The first phase of life, which ranges from age 12 until twenty five years of age (Brahmacharya Ashrama), emphasizes celibacy, perfecting health (physical), developing moral character (psychological), learning cultural etiquettes in respecting others, sacrificing personal pleasures (social) and remaining focused on the greatest priority, education (studentship).

Learning in Hindu tradition

Learning in Hindu tradition is not just gathering information to become pseudo-independent, get a job and economic prosperity but the pursuit of wisdom. Pleasure, comfort, distraction and sexuality are prohibited due to their juxtaposition to sublimation. Brahmacharya is psychologically and biologically the most conducive period to learn the art and skills of self-management. Learning to convert raw energy, impulses and desires into socially constructive outlets cannot be deferred until the adulthood and also cannot be expected to be suddenly integrated during the elderly years. Successful sublimation is a life long process and the earlier one starts the greater the promise of mastery.

In Hindu tradition, this is accomplished by not pressuring the child to prematurely rush into growing up, by providing multiple role modeling by all the significant others (as opposed to the western "trial and error" learning approach,) by allowing the child to remain in the "child mode" for extended period, and surrendering ego to the hierarchy of elders, wise men, family and community. Also importa nt are the cultural values, such as the world is but one big family, along with pursuing wisdom over materials, attachments, pleasures, and the focus on "I", "Me", and "Mine". Cleverness, manipulation, self-centeredness, selfishness, arrogance, argumentativeness, defiance, indulgence in negatives like sex, drugs and cigarettes, are taboos. In this structured, rather basic and simple blue print, the child, adolescent and young adult is expected to perfect his/her first twenty-five years. S(h)e is not allowed to be a capitalist(motivated by money), consumer or materialistic being.

Grihastha Ashrama

The second phase, Grihastha, covers the period of the next twenty-five years. In reality, physical age is flexible depending on life circumstances. For example, if the family has no breadwinner, then it is incumbent upon the young to sacrifice education and be the wage earners, or, in other circumstances, to marry at a younger age for family reasons. Respect, obedience, and sacrifice are among the essential ingredients of Hindu vocabulary.

Grihastha Ashrama recognizes the humans' biological, psychological and social needs. That includes engaging in sexual pleasure in marriage, procreation, earning and accumulating wealth. It also recognizes that elders and parents must be cared and provided for at the same time one must do the same for his or her own children. In Hindu culture, it is thus rather common that three generations live together as an extended or joint family (This often includes siblings and their families.)

Since it is viewed as the most crucial and central phase in Hindu tradition, Grihastha Ashram presents the greatest challenges, testing endurance, resilience, and one's abilities. Due to the nature of roller coaster reality and having to deliver in the face of limitations, it is a most stressful phase (ashrama). Fortunately, the proverb "It takes a village to raise a child" is practiced in Hindu society. The resources, responsibilities, discipline, modeling, and crises management are all shared. This endeavor is neither perfect nor idealistic, but this author (psychologist) has not found a better alternative.

Grihastha Ashram, in spite of engagement in sexual pleasures, materialistic entanglements and permission to experience hedonism, leaves one aspiring and fantasizing for a change. One waits for a break until the appropriate age and time wherein one has fulfilled his moral, social, familial, and professional obligations. How can one move on unless (s)he has paid all his debts, raised children to become productive self-sufficient adults and cared for his/her elders until the day they die? Twenty-five years may not be long enough to meet all the expected challenges and, therefore, Grihastha may have to be extended. In Grihastha, it is imperative that one has resolved, if not totally fulfilled one's biological and sexual needs.

Vanaprastha

The next phase of Vanaprastha cannot begin unless one is ready to take the sublimation to a higher level of transcendence, the pursuit of serving (Sewa) the larger society and spirituality. The risk of becoming corrupt, deviant or sociopathic is much higher if one has not gone through the nitty gritty experiences of the Grihastha phase. Perhaps one of the many reasons of failure (in the sexual acting out) of some other organized religions appears to be rooted in their continued psycho-socio-economic entanglements, ulterior motives and pragmatic approach in terms of demonizing other religions, degrading others' way of life and proselytizing. Sublimation demands absolute motivational objectivity, emotional neutrality and maximum simplicity of action. The process of sublimation can be defined as converting raw energy, aggression, sexuality, instincts, impulses into refined thoughts, feelings and actions which will nurture, support, benefit larger society and in essence entire creation. Every aspect of Hindu Dharma is geared toward this single goal from Birth to Moksha.

Vanaprastha Ashram covers the period of twenty-five years ranging from ages 51-76. In Sanskrit, Vanaprastha literally means departure for the jungle or retiring to the forest. "Jungle" is a metaphor for taking inventory of personal dharma, solitude, detachment, disengagement and relinquishing "I," "Me" and "Mine." When one is ready to let go one's ego, one can truly become free. From birth, a Hindu is expected to realize this and work hard during every phase of life to relinquish it. Ego is viewed as the source of ignorance, and ignorance is considered the source of all suffering. Ego is inseparable from capitalism, as it has become the trademark of individuality in the West. To retain or embrace ego and to operate from it, in the perspective of Hindu psychology, is sheer masochism and spiritual suicide.

Vanaprastha phase, in a superficial way, is similar to retirement in the West. But unlike the capitalistic society, the person does not seek engagement nor spends his life long acquired wisdom in playing golf/ bingo, filling time with hobbies, baby sitting or returning to part time earning.

Western Thinking of Retirement

Western style retirement is conducive to perpetuating capitalism by remaining a consumer and it does not demand full time pursuit of spirituality and a dramatic departure from the usual and mundane. If Hinduism is detachment than Christianity and the West is continued involvement during retirement. However, it does keep one in Karma Yoga (action), which is not inferior to the other methods, such as Bhakti (devotion) or Raja (meditation). What meditation is to India, action is to the West. The routine life from birth to adulthood tends to keep oneself engaged in perpetual problem solving (reactivity) and meeting imposed and expected challenge by constant sympathetic nervous system arousal. In other words, engagement is bound by perpetual anticipations and expectations and thus living on a roller coaster (Sympathetic Nervous System/fight-flight) Thus one does not truly get to quit the rat race other than the breaks on holidays or vacations and Martini lunches and Happy hours. For westerners it's a constant struggle to do it all from Monday to Friday and then from Friday to Sunday recover. Surviving stress becomes the primary preoccupation.

The Rat Race

The rat race is not conducive to the wellbeing of the body, balancing mind, spiritual pursuits or to concentrated introspection. One cannot truly be out of the "mud" and one cannot go far with both feet stuck in it. Vanaprastha promotes and requires initiating the process of separation (distance) from the familiar and ordinary, attachment and desire, and the conditioning-based living and acting reacting. That process is completed in Sanyasa Ashram (renunciation), which follows Vanaprastha phase.

Unfortunately, increasingly larger numbers of people are choosing to stay engaged, prolonging in the rat race and remaining attached to desires, addictions, and financial incentives. Not just in the West, India too has fallen to the culture of hoarding, acquiring and the feeling it is never enough (discontentment). Unfortunately the compulsion is being practiced by using any means, scrupulous or not, to justify obsession with money, materials, property, power and control. It is the curse of the 21st century and has become the modus operandi of modern people. The realization of its price often comes with a health crisis, emotional trauma breakdown of the family and loss of respect by the younger generation. The decline in moral values and the perversion of all the things that encouraged us to rise above becomes a common reality. Consuming is morbid and serving is divine.

Concept of Freedom

Concept of Freedom really means freedom from fear. Vanaprastha is the antidote to the destructive feelings of fear, insecurity, worries, jealousy, inadequacy and doom and gloom. It is often said that we do not use more than one percent of our brains. The challenges and stresses of raising a family, holding on to a job, and dealing with the pressures of being an immigrant or living in another culture are obviously very consuming and sometime overwhelming.

So one can look forward to an early start of Vanaprastha and a socially acceptable way of redesigning one's personal and social blue print for a better living and creating a different milieu and priorities. The retraction of the senses from the external to the internal is also called upon to neutralize the cognitive and emotional exacerbation to which we are subjected. The harnessing of the unfocused, multidimensional, multidirectional waste of energy can now be funneled into the Sewa and meditation process. The stillness that holds the key to spirituality can now become possible.

One can even go so far as to engage in routine fasting and mouna-vrata (practicing silence). These powerful techniques can be called upon to break the cycle of action-reaction based helpless living. Personal growth requires such a stillness and simplicity. Out of the eight steps of Sankhya-Yoga, Yama (psychological discipline), Niyama (body discipline), Asana (body training), and Pranayama (breath training) are conducive to practice during the Grihastha. However, the practice of Dharana, Dhyana and Samadhi requires the context of Vanaprastha, particularly if one is living in western societies where life is busy, constantly interrupted, and the pressures of work and finances just do not dissipate. The cognitive and emotional overload requires a threshold and process at some point in life and Vanaprastha is the perfect bridge. Samadhi is the final step in Sankhya-Yoga and its aim is to cease all identifications, polarizations, duality, ambivalences, action-reactions.

One of the sayings many psychologists use with their patients is that paradox of therapy: Nothing changes and everything changes. Similarly, in Vanaprastha, one is in the "mud" but also out of it through altered feelings, transformed cognition, and a changed life style. What can be more rewarding than to say, "I met all the challenges life threw my way and now I am walking away while I am still ahead in the game?" The younger generation benefits by having more options and opportunity to fill your shoes and to provide leadership to the family as well as to social organizations. Letting go is the essence of Vanaprastha, a challenge to fear, clinging and finding safety in the obsolete and the familiar.

One cannot experience this in its purity until one has relinquished the layers of negative feelings, desires, imaginations, mind racing, negative thoughts and above all, illusions and confusions. Vanaprastha is the most conducive phase in which to seek distance, mental and emotional objectivity. The Bhagavad Gita in essence summarized the secret of happiness as living life without anticipations and expectations: In other words, learning to be content with the occurring experience in the moment. Visualize living without obsessing with roles, goals, achievements, responsibilities and accountabilities. Imagine being free from any and all compulsions: to accomplish that goal one needs to feel secure internally and externally. Such a mindset promotes homeostasis and can ensure good health, particularly after fifty years of age when the risk of decline is greater.

Vanaprastha provides freedom from group dependence and peer pressure thereby freeing the person from the increasing prospect of solitude. It also facilitates acquisition of one's personal dharma (Swadharma). To become spiritual, one has to distance onself from unproductive and unnecessary interpersonal interactions and from the "games people play." This is not a matter of being asocial or anti-social. The sublimation component of Vanaprastha requires that he/she redirects fifty-percent of energy and resources in the service of community and society. Hindu tradition clearly prescribes that such social service (Sewa) and giving (charity) must be without discrimination and ulterior motives of name, fame, or reward (Nishkama Sewa).

On the other hand, one is also responsible for determining the qualifications of the recipient. Charity should serve the targeted need (food, shelter, clothing education, medication, treatment) of the recipient and it must go to the deserving person. Giving money and not knowing whether it will be used to acquire illegal substances or items or support bad habits is taboo. The Giver is ultimately responsible for making sure that he or she will not unwittingly abet crime, violence, exploitation, addictions, exploitations or manipulations.

Vanaprastha need not be restricted to spiritual pursuit since it lies ahead in the next ashrama--Sanyasa, covering the age from seventy-five onward to death. Vanaprastha remains the bridge that connects the Sanyasa and Grihastha. The river that flows under this bridge mandates that persons contribute to social welfare and community well being, ultimately to national/global betterment. What can be more exciting than to dispense all acquired knowledge and experience, resources and good will?

Hindus in the West

Hindus in the West remain in an enviable position as they retire with honors, accomplishments, wealth and worldly knowledge. They are free from the corruption of the Third World kind and can be trusted to provide leadership and accountability at its best. Non-resident Indians (NRIs), persons of Indian origin (PIOs), immigrants, and overseas Indian citizens (OICs) probably offer the richest pool of professional and financial resources to not only rebuild India but revive the Indian Diaspora and take the challenge of global upliftment. Fortunately, the choices are abundant; one can find one's favourite project, institution, venue, and religious, secular, social or governmental organization to join in serving the need and cause.

Many Vanaprasthas are establishing hospitals and schools in their villages in India and abroad. Others are supporting institutions such as One Teacher Schools and Care for the Elderly. Much more remains needing attention such as HIV/AIDS, sexual exploitation of children, the plight of sex workers, child labor, poverty, polio, violence, pollution, and other social and environmental ills. Other concerns, such as demoralization, depression, suicides, domestic violence, racial discrimination, unemployment, and culturally destructive proselytization by missionaries, exist in epidemic proportions in parts of India as well as in nations like Fiji, Uganda, Kenya, Tanzania, Nepal, Trinidad, Guyana, and Suriname.

The Vanaprastha phase offers a rather unique opportunity as well as a challenge to redefine extended family and reach beyond one's biologically significant others. Vanaprasthas are in the position to become the Mahatma Gandhi, Swami Dayananda, Swami Vivekananda and Guru Nanak of the future Indian Diaspora. The world respects the strong and it feeds on the weak. Vanaprasthas have the power to turn the tide and give back the pride to their communities as well as Mother India.

Some secularists worry about accommodating Indian Muslims or Christians in their social work. But they fail to recognize in their enthuasism that these communities have abundant financial, organizational and tactical resources supplied by not only individuals but also corporations and governments. When the US Congress sends its Commission on International Religious Freedom to investigate other nations, it is not looking for what Christians are doing to tribal villages in the North-East India and elsewhere. Assam has become the playground for the most violent of the militant Christians who kidnap, rape, force feed beef, disrupt Hindu festivities and ceremonies. This has been reported by many reporters (Sushanta Talukdar, Francois Gauthiere, David Frawley). The U.S Commission, under the disguise of protecting religious rights of all individuals, is really interested in ensuring the unhindered success of Christian leadership and their missionaries, and it brings to task any government or individuals who might be obstructing proselytization.

Vanaprastha is the pivot upon which the destiny of Hindus revolves. Vanaprasthas have a choice to become the defenders of the motherland, serve the Indian Diaspora or go global. The Vanaprastha does not impose restrictions on the individual's choice of methods, targeted population or cause one wants to serve. Also of no matter to him/her is the organization with which you are affiliated in your service to humankind so long as you exercise discrimination and discipline in giving and at the same time making sure that deserving and qualified recipients are benefiting from your service and offering.

Christians are expected to give ten percent of their income as a tithe. Islam mandates 2.5% of annual income for Zakat (involuntary contribution).

Hindus do not have any such provision due to their non-materialistic approach to religion/Dharma. I suggest Hindus in their Vanaprastha vow to contribute twenty-five percent of their time, skills, and money. Anything less than that will only delay the recovery of the Indian Diaspora, jeopardizing the well being, image and health of our future generations and safety of our vulnerable communities.

When we experience discrimination or read reports of hate crime against Indians, or when, for example, Jersey City gangs target Hindu women because they put Bindi (dot-busting) on their foreheads. We are reminded of how we have collectively failed in acquiring a positive self-image. We have neglected to earn the respect of other communities, not intentionally, but unwitting. We often give the impression of acting clannish or socially incompetent thereby evoking wrong perceptions, hostility or jealousy about ourselves. If we left our image formation to others by default, it will likely be negative and therefore dangerous. We must not overlook institutionalized instances of injustice against Hindus in Pakistan, Uganda, Fiji, Trinidad and Guyana.

Vanaprastha in the Western Context

- Nothing is seen as sacred in the western context. Everything is based on reason and processed by pragmatic dynamics. Consumption and obsession drive human behavior, which sabotage spirituality. Vanaprastha offers the opportunity and tools for a NRI, PIO, or OIC to become purpose-driven, spiritually rooted and to serve the greater cause.
- Insecurity, worrying, fear and constant pressure to keep up with daily challenges become a full time job in the western context. Westerners seem to be always short on time and feel the need to constantly rank or negotiate priorities. Vanaprastha allows one to feel free, live simply, and pursue the ideal of service to others.
- Western context requires sense-based interaction and existence. Reality is dominated by what one sees, feels, hears, tastes, thinks or anticipates. Vanaprastha can successfully facilitate living and the experience of life that is based on intuition and the practice of meditation. Sensory-based living tends to be reactive and leavs the sympathetic nervous system exhausted. The Vanaprastha learns to live through the parasympathetic nervous system, non-reactivity, detached action and emotional neutrality. There is nothing to control, nobody to impress, no hidden agenda or the need for an

ulterior motive. One does not have to do more, try harder and farther. One merely allows everything to happen.

- Unlike the Western push to change things, improve the surrounding milieu; pursue bigger and better goals, in the stage of Vanaprastha one can choose to become free from possessions, desires, and narrow parochial loyalties. One can start preparing or living for what one always wanted to do--be free. Detachment, contentment and visualizing the state of being in nothingness are powerful concepts to promote ultimate well being.
- If one never had a happy place, happy phase or happy time, the Vanaprastha offers another chance to re-examine it all and start afresh. It frees us from the obligation to be needed, approved or defined. It allows one to begin laying the groundwork for freedom. In Vanaprastha, one prepares toward Sanyasa, not necessarily to be a monk and live in holy places. One can merely practice Sanyasa where one is. Sanyasa is a full-time pursuit of spirituality and Moksha for self or others.
- In the West, one starts out having to meet expectations and be restrained in youth, following through with one's family and social obligations and involvements. In Vanaprastha, however, one gets a chance to redefine the meaning, purpose, direction, priorities, self, others, and even religiosity. One is permitted to shrug off the old and resume a new identity or even relinquish all identities given or chosen.
- Vanaprastha is synonymous to making a difference internally or externally, personally or socially, resigning or restarting, and even all of it at once. Absent is the status quo, stagnation or just getting by. Vanaprastha offers the opportunity and means to rise above the mundane and maintenance.
- Midpoint in life does not have to be midlife crises. With some awareness and realization, it can be a high time for sublimation. Sexuality has to be put in its proper place around this time since it offers a rather limited means to become intimate and experience joy. The desires will only lead to frustration and therefore one need to be open to experience a higher level of maturity, one not based on senses but rather on consciousness, balance and mindfulness.
- One can afford to become the roving ambassador of service and good will by visiting various countries and attempting to make the world a better place than was first encountered.

Prescriptins and proscriptions in Vanaprastha

1. Changing the perception of time, people, places, and context is crucial. The everyday world of people and places where all the economic, social, and emotional drama takes place is not conducive to Vanaprastha. Distance from the familiar and routine places such as family, work, business and socialization is required. Interacting in the society in which one lived his/her earlier phases must be cuŗta iled significantly. If one desires less, or even better nothing, the potential for contentment increases multifold. Desire for Hindus is the single most threatening element as it triggers somato-psycho-socio-spiritual crisis (vicious cycle of like-dislike, clinging-aversion, pleasure-pain, etc). As long as one pursues people, things, objects, stimuli, and allows attachment, one is doomed to suffer from endless chain of insecurity, depression, vulnerability, anxiety, worrying, and obsessivity.

2. If necessary, one may return to the household one left behind from time to time. One can even resume one's place back in the family, work and society if one chooses to relinquish Vanaprastha.

3. Wife may accompany husband in Vanaprastha and follow with him the same routine. The sexual dimension of the relationship must be moderated but not given up as in Sanyasa.

4. Ideally the dwelling place should be away from the neighborhoods, the hut being simple and built with plants and covered with leaves. This is open to modification in accordance to time, place and person.

5. Fancy clothes, costly fabric, and customized tailoring must be avoided. Clothes should be made of vegetable fibers, honoring simplicity and autonomy. Nature was our original home and now we get another chance to return to it.

6. Food should be vegetarian, simple, mostly consisting of plants, fruits and vegetables. The root and stem vegetables shaped like bulbs are to be avoided (this author failed to find any rationale or justification for this directive). One should consume one meal a day, never completely filling the stomach. One must make sure, before eating, that no one in sight is hungry. It is one's duty to invite a hungry person, whether friend or foe. Alcohol and drugs are an absolute taboo in Vanaprastha.

7. Meditation, contemplation, good reading and yoga should occupy all available leisure time. However, gardening is not prohibited.

8. Adequate time should be spent in teaching, helping, supporting and nurturing others in hospitals, schools, orphanages, Gurukul and other appropriate social service settings. Attaching to a temple to offer specialized services is also recommended.

9. Emphasis on rituals is negligible while serving society since it is the more important mission along with meditation, contemplation, silence, and acquiring knowledge.

10. Possessiveness for land, gold and women has to be avoided. Ambition, desire, honors, wealth, and luxury must be curtailed. All nonessential money matters must be restricted.

11. Frugality, simplicity, and contentment are essential traits to be practiced.

12. Restraining anger, relinquishing pride, and subordinating all negative feelings are essential in the Vanaprastha's life. Buddha viewed anger as one of the three poisons along with greed and delusion. Non-reactivity is the ultimate strength of a model Vanaprastha. Detaching from the anger holds the key. Emotions of compassion and equanimity are cultivated.

13. Yajna is approved but sacrificing any living thing as part of the Havan is not acceptable. Havan is essential to the practice of Dharma-making oblations/offerings through the fire pit. It is also psychologically a very meaningful ritual as it facilitates group meditation, symbolic detachment/giving away and ensures that all prayers are directed for the well being of all living things in the entire universe. Regardless of its appearance it is a highly secular ritual and common in many ancient traditions worldwide.

For a Hindu, the above list of distinctions, the do's and don'ts, should not bring any surprises since most of us have grown with these values and practices. A good number of us have lived our entire lives guided by these principles of simplicity, frugality, avoiding materialism, curbing desire, greed and seeking possessions. During our Grihastha, we aggressively went after wealth, success, and possessions, to prove a point that we are as good as anybody else. It was a challenge and most of us met it. Now the challenge is to walk away from it all and to return it where it came from. The best way is to serve society, do charity, and to teach the wisdom and professional expertise to the younger generations. In addition to the social benefits, this task prevents a sense of loss of meaning, purpose and impending boredom. In the West, depression, dementia and drinking are pervasive among elderly population. Gone are the insecurities and the need for compliments, tokens and trophies, leaving every action with the potential for immense possibilities and great sense of fulfillment. Choices are numerous and one should choose the cause which best suits one's temperament, personality, faith and expertise.

The challenge of the Vanaprastha phase is not that it may not be kept, but that there is something inherently demanding in the institution of Vanaprastha. The greatest challenge is continued need for attachment, and unresolved sensual passions. Other complications include the risk of making abrupt decisions, choosing methods incompatible with one's temperament, or acting prematurely before having met all his/ her social, familial, and financial obligations. Above all, the greater challenge is not knowing what Vanaprastha entails. This can be managed by allowing sufficient time for planning and preparing, discussing and comparing notes with those who are already in the Vanaprastha stage. Sharing with the family and allowing at least five to ten years to develop a customized blueprint will ease entry into Vanaprastha. A well thought out plan should prevent failure, disappointments or regrets.

Unlike Sanyasa, one does not have to be religious or fixated on Moksha. Vanaprastha phase involves distancing oneself from the world to a retreat in order to redirect, take inventory, practice letting go and to figure out the answer to "what now?" after half a century of struggling, living, learning, proving, competing, giving, taking,, accommodating, and performing.

As an ihe ideal the stage of Vanaprastha is generic; it allows you to design your own time, place, and context. You may choose to enter it later or earlier. You may prefer to do social service or just spend your time worshipping in the temple. You may choose to go and live in an adult community. Someone else may decide to live in Haridwar (a holy city in India). I may decide to hop between adult community (in USA or India) or the holy cities and social service in far away countries.

It is not as much what you will do as what you should consider giving up--like the rat race, automated style of living, being consumed by desire for earning and acquiring more, and the desparate fighti to hold on to what you have hoarded. The society we live in is insane because of the stress, demands, challenges, and unpredictability that we have to put up with. Prosperity is infused with cruelty, insanity, exploitation, and insecurity, which produces alcoholism, crime, suicides, depression, divorce, child abuse, and angst. Increasing modernization and prosperity have brought greater insecurity and vulnerability along with pervasiveness of pathology.

Progress can only occur when changes are made consciously, simultaneously and are all-inclusive. Living well is probably the most difficult human endeavor because learning to live also incorporates learning to die. Since cause and effect are inseparable, karma is human destiny. We can create peace, love, justice, fairness, and harmony. We can also aspire to become world citizens, universal human beings and leaders of spirituality. For that, we do not need more wealth nor do we need more territories. Let us seek sanity inside and out. Vanaprastha offers a useful context and platform to attain these goals.

Chapter 8

Report on vānaprastha varga, Bloomington, IL camp July 24-31, 2005

[Shrinarayan Chandak, Vimal Patel, and Pukhraj Jain]

During the next few years, over twenty thousand Indians who immigrated to the US in the 1960s are expected to retire. Nestled on the shore of beautiful Lake Bloomington near Bloomington, IL, the picturesque East bay campsite turned out to be an ideal location for about a dozen elderly Hindus living in the United States and Canada who met there from July 24-31, 2005 to discuss (1) the specific problems the retiring Hindu Americans would face and (2) how they could contribute creatively and positively to the welfare of the growing Indian community in America.

The participants at the varga received judicious guidance and advice from K.P. Sudarshanji, Sarasanghachalak of the RSS and other Sangha dignitaries including Professor Ved Nanda and Shri Shankar Tattvavadi. Valuable comments and suggestions also came from Jeff Armstrong (Kavindra), Guruvarya Sahebji of Anoopam Mission and Swamiji Krishnamaniji Maharaj, Navatanpuridham, Gujarat based in India. The following report is based on the input received from these dignitaries as well as from following participants who attended the varga: Shri Janardan Bhatt, Asha and Shrinarayan Chandak, Ramesh Chitnis, Shridhar Damle, Anita and Uday Deoskar, Keshav Dixit, Shri Goel, Bithal Gujarati, Pukhraj Jain, Shrikant Kalvade, Shrimati Malpani, Vasant Pandav, Vimal Patel, Ram Sastry, Ramdev Sood, and Shrinivas Tilak.

At the end of deliberations on the first day, an ad hoc committee comprising of Shri Shrinarayan Chandak, Pukhraj Jain, Vimal Patel, and Shrinivas Tilak was formed to prepare an interim report based on the key themes that were expected to emerge during discussions on subsequent days. The report below is based on over forty-five items that were suggested by participants emerged as being most important to them (see appendix I) and which were divided into six broader categories for facilitating discussion: (1) Ethico-religious, (2) socio-cultural, (3) legal, (4) political, (5) economic, and (6) academic/educational (see appendix for the categories and the list of items proposed during this meeting).

Introduction

Pain and suffering (whether physical, psychological, emotional, existential, social, or metaphysical) are universal human phenomena. World cultures and religions provide numerous accounts of how to explain or make suffering meaningful and/or how to transcend it. Suffering is explained to be self-inflicted or inflicted by an external agency or factors, including even a spiritual or cosmic force. It is located in the body, mind, self or more widely dispersed within the web of social relations. It may be accepted passively as social obligation or fate or it may be actively resisted as an obstacle to human fulfillment.

While disease destroys the wholeness and integrity of the body, the pain and suffering threaten the very existence of the person. Aging portends more than mere biological decay. Suffering begins when an impending destruction of one's person is discerned. It will continue until the threat of disintegration has passed or until the integrity of the person is restored in some other manner. In the case of old age and aging, however, the threat will not pass. Then how to deal with the threat of suffering precipitated by the onslaught of old age that will only end in death? In the Indian tradition Dharma provides a variety of possible solutions. (See introduction for details.)

The ideal Hindu American elderly

The participants agreed that in Indian history the problem of old age was successfully handled and that model can be used in USA (see apendix II). Viewing aging as a career provides an alternative to the typically modern conception that growing old is simply a series of losses to be endured. On the contrary, it introduces the idea that although losses do occur with the passing of years, gains are clearly accrued as well. However, these gains are not equally distributed to all, and the analogy to a career in its everyday sense of the meaning suggests the idea of differential success. In every society, the rewards possible in old age depend largely on the individual ability, resourcefulness, good judgment, and luck during the life cycle.

Creating vānprastha activists in the USA

The creed of the modern day Hindu American vānaprastha activist would be: Where there is a need; there is a role for the vānaprastha (*jahan kam vahan hum*). Toward that objective it was decided to prepare (1) a primer "American vānaprasthas as agents of change," (2) a short refresher course based on (a) the ideal of the Karmayogi outlined in the Gītā and (b) the theory and practice of Gandhian Satyagraha for training vānaprasthas as social activists. They will be trained to operate as self-motivated and concerned senior citizens able to initiate projects in specific fields locally without much oversight or supervision. It will be inculcated in them that the power and strength of activism lies in decentralization. Not all accomplished activists and leaders are born that way. Such skills have to be consciously cultivated and developed. Volunteer vānaprasthas will be invited to take an inventory of the following skills. Counseling will be offered in the following areas: organization building, public speaking, citizen lobbying, research and policy analysis, media and press relations, meeting facilitation, event planning and management, computer and information systems, formal and informal networking.

The proposed primer will discuss how to form small cadres and networks of vānaprasthas and train them to act in providing help and support in the following areas: (1) Ethico-religious activism; (2) Socio-cultural activism,; (3) Political activism; (4) Economic activism; (5) Legal activism; (6) Healthcare advocacy; and (7) Academic and media advocacy.

Ethico-religious activism

Volunteers will be trained to teach yoga and mediation, Hindu samskāras and education, Service of Hindu Americans and others (*sevā*), and consolidating Hindu Americans (*sanghatan*)

Socio-cultural activism

Volunteers will learn how to identify and address the typical social and family problems of the American Hindu society and devising ways of helping them through the vānaprastha movement. Others will learn how to connect theoretical learning to meaningful community service and social work. They will aid recent immigrants from India who have had difficulty adapting to American culture and learning to speak English.

Other tasks would include (1) identifying needs of Hindu Americans and generating resources for creating a healthy socio-cultural life style for Hindu communities in the US; (2) fostering community relations (*samparka*), community building (*samgraha*), and community improvement (*samskāras*), community organization (*sanghatan*); (3) creating organizations and fulfilling the needs of the Hindu Society in America, addressing their needs through such efforts, each vānaprastha will strive to become an organization in himself addressing some aspects and need of the society

Political activism

In contrast to the philosophy of disengagement, active participation of the vānaprasthas will be advocated in the ongoing societal and governmental process and other positions of social and political responsibility. They will be encouraged to join the two main political parties viz the republican and the Democratic and attend annual conventions at the federal, state, and local levels as delegates where they will strive to lobby for causes that will help Hindu Americans in different fields. Vānaprasthas will strive to found HAARP--Hindu American Association of Retired Persons to further the interests of Hindu Americans who have retired.

Economic activism

Vānaprastha volunteers with background in industry, finance, and management will train others on how to enlist cooperation of their community's banking network to finance activities related to our cause. In the USA the Community Reinvestment Act (CRA) requires banks to publish the number of loans granted or denied, neighborhood to neighborhood. It obligates bank to grant a percentage of its loans to people in the community in which it is located. Volunteers will train suitable Hindu candidates on how to attract funding for their worthy causes. Others will act as fund raisers and secure loans from banks and other financial institutions.

Legal activism

Vānaprastha volunteers will engage in seeking satisfactory resolution of numerous problems of legal nature faced by Hindu Americans: These will include immigration, adoption of children born in India, preparation and execution of the living will, elderly and other forms abuse, domestic violence, discrimination in social, economic, and religious matters. Others will work in close collaboration with Hindu American Foundation.

Healthcare advocacy

Volunteers will be encouraged and helped offering healthcare services based on āyurvedic principles. Others will open Adult Day Health Care centers where neighborhood senior citizens with difficulties such as frailty, alienation and boredom will be helped. They will be paired with students in order that each gets to know his or her new friend through oral-history interviews, arts and crafts, and general socializing. Social movements and interest groups shape welfare state outcomes. Welfare state programs spawn large, active constituencies that exert political pressure to maintain or expand their programs. Nowhere does this seem as likely as with Social Security and Medicare, the two largest social welfare programs in the United States.

Academic and media advocacy

Vānaprastha volunteers with background in the academia will be encouraged to establish an ongoing relationship with individual professors who teach India and Hinduism related courses in schools, colleges, and universities. Retired Hindu academic in collaboration with Hindu students maintain active presence on American campuses along with the members of the local chapter of the Hindu Students' Council. Their activities will involve assuring balanced presentation of India and Hinduism by (a) collecting course outlines of relevant courses offered on the campuses of their local university and assessing them for balanced presentation of Hinduism and India; (b) establishing ongoing relationship with area reference librarians and those who order, acquire, and catalogue books on Hinduism; (c) attending doctoral dissetations on India and Hinduism related subjects by candidates; (d) attending lectures by experts who are on the lecture circuit and raising issues or questions of particular concern to us; (e) opening weekly service for benefit of Hindu students in cooperation with campus chaplaincy services; (f) writing critical reviews of books for Amazon.com or Barnes & Noble etc.

Those with experience in the media and public relations will develop rapport with reporters and columnists working in their areas. Volunteers will operate as a source of reliable and informed Hindu position and perspective on a host of issues that arise in thlpublic arena almost daily. They will also strive to create the circumstances and media events to draw attention to issues of particular concerns to Hindus everywhere.

Appeal to Hindu Americans

After you have read the report, write us back giving your input indicating how you could help us attain the dual goal of the typical Hindu American vānaprasthas: (1) self realization and (2) welfare of the Hindu American community. We are exploring the possibility of holding a conference of interested Hindu Americans from all walks of life and belonging to different age groups to establish HAARP—Hindu American Association of Retired Persons. Please write to us (i.e. to individual coordinators) about what you consider should be agenda for such a conference and how you would like to help us in making it a success.

Please send your responses to Srinarayan Chandak at chandak101@yahoo.com

Appendix I

Priority items suggested for discussion at vānaprastha varga: Bloomington, IL 2005

(Based on each participant picking an issue that was most important)

Priority Requester	Issue	Comment
Shrikant Kalvade	Hindu Unity / Identity (based on sādhāraṇa dharma)	Make this to be the overall Objective of the group
Bithal Gujrati	Facilitate marital opportunities for Hindus	Facilitate matrimonial alliances Among newly arriving eligible Hindu single men and women
Pukhraj Jain	Prepare Hinduism/Dharma 101 course	Create source material to teach A course on Dharma 101
Janardan Bhatt	Train counselers for Hindu youth	Prepare material on preventive and corrective advice and counseling based on needs of Hindu youth
Uday Deoskar	Prepare informative material on old age living	Consider all relevant aspects of old age living
Ram Sastry, Shrinivas Tilak	Create Hindu American Association of Retired Persons (HAARP)	Def.: HAARP-USA is a Hindu VP organization that seeks to promote interest of VPs in harmony with larger community
Ramdev Sood	Facilitate interaction with other senior clubs	Comment: An activity of HAARP
Asha Chandak, Srinarayan Chandak	Facilitate the process of adopting Hindu children (agency etc)	Further Investigation needed
Vasant Pandav	Operate daycare centers for Hindu children	Awaiting results of item 47
Ramesh Chitnis	Reach out to Native	Deferred until more information

	Americans	Becomes available
Ramesh Chitnis	Engage programmer to develop vānaprastha skills and satisfy their needs; prepare survey and questionnaire	Assign a team to develop appropriate document
Anita Deoskar	Make available educational material (audio-visual media) eg. Ekatmata mantra	Collect required materials
Ramdev Sood, Shrinivas Tilak, Srinarayan Chandak	Identify literature relating to vānaprastha needs and circulate	Should become an activity of HAARP

Appendix II

The ideal Hindu American elderly

A proper response to the experience of growing old in today's North America for Hindus would be neither resignation nor continuation of middle age norms, but the adoption of values and projects different from those appropriate for youth and middle age. Against activism, we should affirm that old age means positive discovery of values and meanings different in character from those accessible to us in youth and middle age. With reference to the value of disengagement and isolation from the world, we need to affirm that insights and values achievable in old age are related to worldly needs and interests and are of direct use to the world at large. In the typical American context, we expect the vānaprasthas to contribute significantly as administrators, teachers, educators, managers, consultants, and activists in areas where they may have acquired considerable expertise.

The notion of differential disengagement of modern gerontology better explains the traditional ideal of the vānaprastha. As explained in a Sanskrit expression (*ātmano mokṣārtham jagat hitāya ca*) it is two fold: (1) self realization and (2) seeking welfare of the larger community. This dual objective of the vānaprastha comes out forcefully in the character of Dhṛtarāṣṭra in the Mahābhārata who immediately after the Great War had suffered from recurrent fits of extreme depression and suicidal tendencies. The process of disengagement, in his case, lasts for fifteen years culminating in a state of calm serenity and a promise of spiritual fulfilment. The notion of differential disengagement helps us understand the traditional Indian view of aging as an opportunity for discovering one's own inner world as a worthy alternative to the external world with which one has been interacting in the first half of one's life. The tempo of the process of disengagement, which can culminate in spiritual maturation and fulfilment, quickens with growing age. It is demarcated with significant changes and transition in the role complex, value structure, and status identity of the aging individual. This can be demonstrated by analyzing select events that occur in Dhṛtarāṣṭra's later life (see the article by Dr Shrinivas Tilak in this volume).

Bibliography

(includes sited as well other recommended works):

Original Works in Sanskrit

The Buddhacarita or Acts of the Buddha (2 vols). 1972. Edited by E.H. Johnston. Delhi: Munshiram Manoharlal.

Chāndogya Upaniṣad [With commentary of Madhva]. 1910. Reprint. Translated by B. D. Basu. New York: AMS Press, 1974.

Carakasamhitā by Agniveśa and revised by Caraka [with commentary by Cakrapāṇidatta. 1941. Bombay: Nirnaysagar Press.

Carakasamhitā [With Āyurvedadīipikā commentary of Cakrapāṇidatta]. 1952. Bombay: Nirnaya Sagar Press.

Dīgha Nikāya [Dialogues of the Buddha]. 3 Parts. 1965. Translated by T. W. Rhys Davids. Sacred Books of the Buddhists translated by various scholars and edited by T. W. Rhys Davids, vols. 2-4. London: Pali Text Society.

Gautama Dharma Sūtram [With Maskarı Bhāṣya].1969. Critically edited by Veda Mitra. Delhi: Veda Mitra & Sons.

Kādambarī. Part 1. 1953. Kashi Sanskrit Texts Series, edited by Krsnamohan Sastri, no. 15. Benares: Chowkhamba Sanskrit Series.

Kālasamuddeśa [Chapter Three of Bhartṛhari's Vākyapadīiyam with Helārāja's commentary].1972. Translated from the Sanskrit by Peri Sarvesvara Sharma. Delhi: Motilal Bāṇa rsidass.

Kāmasūtram [With the commentary Jayamangalā].1929. Edited by Sri. Goswami Damodara Shastri. Benares: Chowkhamba.

Kirātārjunīiyam. 6 Parts.1965. Edited by Janardana Sastri. Delhi: Motilal Banarsidass.

Mahābhārata. 30 vols.1933-1960. Critically edited by V.S. Sukhthankar et al. Poona: Bhandarkar Oriental Research Institute.

Majjhima Nikāya [The Collection of the Middle Length Sayings]. 3 vols. 1954-1959. Reprint. Translated by I. B. Horner. Pali Texts Translation Society Series, no.s 29, 30, 31. London: Luzac & CO.

Manu Smṛti [With the Commentary Manvārtha Muktāvali of Kullūka].1946. 10th ed. Edited by Narayana Ram Acharya, Kavyatirtha. Bombay: Nirnaya Sagar Press.

The Mīmāmsā Nyāya Prakāśa or Āpādevī: A treatise on the Mīimāmsā System by Āpadeva.1986. Translated into English by Franklin Edgerton. Delhi: Sri Satguru Publications (first published 1929).

Milindapanha [The Questions of King Milinda]. 2 vols. 1890. Reprint. Translated by T. W. Rhys Davids. Sacred Books of the East Series, translated by various scholars and edited by F. Max Muller, nos. 35, 36. Delhi: Motilal Banarsidass. 1969.

Mīmāmsā Paribhāṣā [of Kṛṣṇa Yajvan]. 1987. Translated into English by Swami Madhavananda, Calcutta: Advaita Ashrama.

Mṛchhakaṭika [Of Śūdraka]. 1924. Reprint. Edited with the Commentary of Prthviraja by M. R. Kale. Bombay: Booksellers Publishing Co.1962.

Nirukta of Yāska [With the Vivṛti]. 1930 Reprint. Critically edited by Mukund Jha Bakshi. Panini Vaidika Granthamala no. 12. New Delhi: Panini.1982.

Pancavimśa Brāhmaṇa [The Brāhmaṇa of Twenty-five Chapters].1931. Edited by W. Caland. Calcutta: Asiatic Society of Bengal.

Ṛgveda Samhitā [With the commentary of Sāyaṇa]. 4 Pts.1936-1946. Edited by N. S. Sontakke et al. Poona: Vaidika Samsodhaka Mandal.

Rāmāyaṇa. 15 vols. Critically edited by G. H. Bhatt and Other Scholars. Baroda: Oriental Research Institute, 1958-

Raghuvamśa. [A Mahākāvya with 19 Cantos with the Commentary of Mallinātha Sūri, edited by Vasudeva Shastri Panasikar with critical & explanatory notes of the text & an essay on the life &

writings of the poet]. Translated by K. M. Joglekar. Bombay: Pandurang Javji, 1925.

Samyutta Nikāya [The Book of the Kindred Sayings]. 5 vols. Translated by Mrs. Rhys Davids & F.ā L. Woodward. London: Pali Text Society, 1951-1956.

Śābara-Bhāşya, vol.1 (Adhyaya I-III). 1973. Translated by Ganganath Jha, Baroda: Oriental Institute.

Śatakatrayam of Bhartṛhari [The Southern Archetype of the Three Centuries of Epigrams ascribed to Bhartrhari]. 1946. Critically edited by D. D. Kosambi with an anonymous Sanskrit Commentary edited by K. V. Krishnamoorthy Sharma. Bharatiya Vidya Series, no. 9. Bombay: Bharatiya Vidya Bhavan.

Śatapatha Brāhmaṇa [of the Mādhyandīna Śākhā]. 1849. Reprint. 2d ed. Edited by Albrecht Weber. The Chowkhambha Sanskrit Series, no. 96. Varanasi: Chowkhambha, 1964.

Saundarananda [of Aśvaghoşa]. 1925. Reprint. Critically edited and translated by E. H. Johnston. Delhi: Motilal Bāṇa rsidass, 1975.

Subhāşita Ratnabhāaṇdāgāra [Gems of Sanskrit Poetry: A Collection of Witty, Epigrammatic, Instructive and Descriptive Verses with their Sources]. 8th ed. Enlarged and re-edited by Narayana Ram Acharya. Bombay: Nirnaya Sagar Press, 1952.

Suśrutasamhitā [With the Commentary of Dalhana].1948. Bombay:Nirnaya Sagar Press.

Sutta-Nipāta [A Collection of Discourses]. 1958. Reprint. Translated from Pali by V. Fausboll. The Sacred Books of the East Series, no. 10. Pt.2. Delhi: Motilal Bāṇa rsidass, 1973.

Taittirīiya Upanişad. 1925. Reprint. Translated by S. C. Vidyaranya & M. L. Sandal. New York: AMS Press, 1974.

Upanişad Samgraha [Containing 188 Upanişads]. 1970. Reprint. Edited with introduction by J. L. Shastri. Delhi: Motilal Banarsidass, 1980.

Vākyapadīyam [Of Bhartṛhari, Part 3.1977. With the Commentary "Prakāśa" by Helārāja]. 2 vols. Edited by Bhagiratha Prasada Tripathi. Saraswati Bhavan Granthamala no. 91. Varanasi: Sampurnananda Samskrit Visvavidyalaya.

Viṣṇudharmottara Purāṇa [Third Khanda].1958. 2 vols. Critically edited with notes by Priyabala Shah. Gaekwad's Oriental Series, nos. 130, 137. Baroda: Oriental Institute.

Yājńavalkya Smṛti [The Institutes of Yājńavalkya together with the Commentary called Mitaksara by Sri Vijnanesvara].1914. Edited by J. R. Gharpure. The Collections of Hindu Law Texts, no.1. 1st ed. Bombay: J. R. Gharpure.

Yogadarśanam [Yoga Sutra of Patañjali with the Yoga Bhasya of Vyāsa, the Tattva Vaiśāradī of Vācaspati Miśra and the Yoga Vārtika of Vijāna Bhiksu]. Varanasi, India: Bharatiya Vidya Prakashan, 1971.

Yogavāsiṣṭha of Vālkimi.1937. [with the Commentary Vasisthamaha Rāmāyaṇa Tatparyaprakasa, Pt. 1]. Edited by Wasudev Laxman Sastri Panasikar. 3rd rev. ed. Edited by Narayana Ram Acarya. Bombay: Nirnaya Sagara Press.

Secondary Works

Agrawala, V. S., 1963. India as Known to Pāṇini: A Study of the Cultural Material in the Aṣṭādhyāyi. 2d ed., rev. & enl. Varanasi: Prithvi Prakashan.

Bhalla, A. and Blackmore, K. 1981. Elders of Ethnic Minority Groups. Birmingham, UK: All Faiths for One Race.

Bhattacharya, Biswanath. 1976. Aśvaghoṣa: A critical study of his authentic Kāvyas, and the apocryphal works, with special reference to his contributions to the classical Sanskrit literature, and his doctrinal standpoint as a Buddhist. Śānti niketan: Visva-Bharati.

Bhattacharya, Biswanath.1969. The Deeds of Harṣa: Being a Cultural Study of Bāṇa 's Harṣa charita. Edited by P. K. Agrawala. Varanasi: Prithvi Prakashan.

Bloomfield, Maurice. 1906. A Vedic Concordance, Reprint. Edited by Charles Lanman. Harvard Oriental Series, vol. 10. Delhi: Motilal Banarsidass, 11.

Breytspraak, Linda. 1984. The Development of Self in Later Life. Boston: Little, Brown & Co.

Callahan, Daniel. 1987. Setting Limits: Medical Goals in Aging Society. New York: Simon & Schuster.

Chapple, Christopher. 1986. Karma and Creativity, Albany, N.Y.: State University of New York Press.

Chari, V. K., 1990. Sanskrit Criticism, Honolulu: University of Hawaii Press.

Chinen, Allan B.1984.Modal Logic, Development, and Wisdom: A New Paradigm of Development and Late Life Potential. Human Development 27 (1984): 42-56.

Childers, James F. 1979. A Right to Health Care. The Journal of Medicine and Philosophy, vol.4, no.2 (1979): 132-147.

Cicirelli, Victor G.1986. A Comparison of Helping Behaviour to Elderly Parents of Adult Children with Intact and Disrupted Marriages. Gerontology: Sponsored by the Gerontological Society of America, edited by Lillian E., 97-122. New York: Springer Publishing Co.

Desai, Prakash. 1989. Health and Medicine in the Hindu Tradition: Continuity and Cohesion. New York: Crossroad.

Deshpande, G. T.1971. Indological Papers, vol. 1. Nagpur: Vidarbha Samshodhan Mandal.

Dhayagude, Suresh, 1981. Western and Indian Poetics: A Comparative Study. Bhandarkar Oriental Series No 16, Bhandarkar Oriental Research Institute, Pune.

Engelhardt, H Tristram. 1979. Is Aging a Disease? In Robert M. Veatch (ed) Life Span: Values & Life-Extending Technologies, 184-194. New York: Harper & Row.

Entralgo, H. In Changing Values in Medicine, edited by Eric J. Casell & Mark Siegler, New York: University Publications of America, 1979).

Gachter, Othmar. 1983. Hermeneutics and Language in Pūrva Mīmāmsā: A Study in Śābara Bhāşya, Delhi: Motilal Banarasidass.

Gadamer, Hans-Georg. 1975. Truth and method. New York: Continuum.

Gadow, Sally. 1986. What does it mean to grow old: refdlections from the humanities. Durham, N.C.: Duke University Press.

Ganguli, Kisari Mohan. 1991. The Mahabharata of Krishna-Dwaipayana Vyasa translated into English Prose from the original Sanskrit text in 12 volumes [1884-96]. New Delhi: Munshiram Manoharlal.

Gonda, Jan.1959. Four Studies in the Language of the Veda. Leiden: E.J. Brill.

Gonda Jan. 1975. Selected Studies: History of Ancient Indian Religions vol. 4. Leiden: E. J. Brill.

Gonda, Jan. 1979. The Medium in the Ṛgveda. Leiden: E.J. Brill.

Gress, Lucille D. & Rose Therese Bahr. 1984. The Aging Person: A Holistic Perspective. St. Louis, Toronto: The C.V. Mosby Co.

Guha, Ranjit.1982. Subaltern Studies I: Writings on South Asian History and Society. Delhi: Oxford University Press.

Guha, Ranjit. 1983. Elementary Aspects of Peasant Insurgency in Colonial India, Delhi: Oxford University Press.

Gurevitch, Z. D.1989. The Power of Not Understanding: The Meeting of Conflicting Ideas. Journal of Behaviourial Science, 25, 2, (May 1989): 165-173.

Gurjar, G. K. 1979. Āyurveda and Code of Right Conduct (sadacara). Nagarjuna, vol.22, no.5 (Jan.1979): 118-123.

Gutman, D. 1960. The Cross-cultural Perspective: Notes toward a comparative psychology of aging. In Handbook of the Psychology of Aging, edited by J.E. Birren and K.W. Schaie, New York: Van Nostrand Reinhold.

Jefferys, Margot ed.1989. Growing Old in the Twentieth Century, London: Routeledge.

Jha, Ganganath.1978. The Prbhākara School of Pūrva Mīmāmsā. Delhi: Motilal Banarasidass 1911.

Jha, Kala Nath, 1975. Figurative Poetry in Sanskrit Literature, Delhi: Motilal Banarasidass.

Kalyanraman, S. 2003. Saraswati Civilization. Bangalore: Babasaheb Apte Smarak Samiti (Volume 7 of 7-volume encyclopaedic work on Sarasvati Civilization).

Kane, P. V., 1968-1978. History of Dharmaśāstra: Ancient & Medieval Religious & Civil Law. 5 Vols. Government Oriental Series Class B, no. 6. Poona: Bhandarkar Oriental Research Institute.

Khosla, Renu.1982. The Changing Familial Role of South-Asian Women in Canada: A Study in Identity Transformation. In Asian Canadians Regional Perspectives: Selections from the Proceedings Asia Canadian Symposium, edited by Victor K.

Ujimoto and Gordon Hirabayashi, 178-184, Guelph, Ont.: University of Guelph.

Kleinman, Arthur. 1980. Patients and healers in the context of culture: an exploration of the borderland between anthropology, medicine, and psychiatry. Berkeley: University of California Press.

Klostermaier, Klaus. 1994. A Survey of Hinduism. Albany, N.Y.: State University of New York Press.

Kosidlak, J.G.1980. Self-help for Senior Citizens. Journal of Gerontology & Nursing. 6 (11) 1980: 663-668.

Krishnamoorthy, K. 1959. (a) Stylistic Repetition in the Veda. Amsterdam: N.V. Noord, Hollandsche Vitgevers Maatschappij.

Krishnamoorthy, K. 1975 (b), A History of Indian Literature: Vedic Literature (Samhitas & Brāhmaṇas). Wiesbaden: Otto Harrassowitz.

Krishnamoorthy, K., 1977. The Vakrokti-Jīvita of Kuntaka: Critically edited with Variants, Introduction and English translation, Dharwad, India: Karnatak University.

Levin, L.S. et al. 1976 Self-care: Lay Initiatives in Health. New York: Prodist.

Ley, Dorothy. 1988 Geriatric Ethics. Synapse 4(1) 1988: 4-7.

Limaye, V. P., 1974. Critical Studies in Mahābhāşya. Hoshiarpur, India

Macdonell, Arthur A. & Arthur O. Keith, 1967. Vedic Index of Names & Subjects. vol. 1. 1912. Reprint. Delhi: Motilal Banrsidass.

McKee, Patrick L. 1982. Philosophical Foundations of Gerontology. New York: Human Science Press.

Mahadevan, T. M. P., 1980. The Hymns of Sankara. Delhi: Motilal Banarasidass.

Mattoo, Amitabh. The Independent. December 19, 1992.

Mhaskar, K.S. and N.S. Watve.1954. Health & Longevity in Āyurveda [in Sanskrit, Hindi and English]. Vol. 2. Bombay: Board of Research in Āyurveda.

Mhaskar, K.S. ed.1954. Svasthavṛttam, [Sanskrit, Hindi, and Marathi] 2 vols. Bombay: Board of Research for Āyurveda.

Naidoo, Josephine, 1982. The South Asian Experience of Aging. In Asian Canadians Regional Perspectives: Selections from the Proceedings Asia Canadian Symposium, edited by Victor K. Ujimoto and Gordon Hirabayashi, 84-95, Guelph, Ont.: University of Guelph.

Naidu, S Baliah. 1988. Religion and Health in the Context of Holistic Medicine. Paper read at the Canadian Society for the Study of religion, annual meeting, Windsor, Ont, May 30-June 2, 1988.

Norman, A.1984.Stressful and Facilitating Life Experiences for South Asian Women in Canada. In Asian Canadians: Aspects of Social Change, edited by Victor K. Ujimoto and Josephine Naidoo, 90-111, Guelph, Ont.: University of Guelph, 1984.

Norman, A, 1985. Triple Jeopardy: Growing Old in a Second Homeland, London: Centre for Policy on Ageing.

Obeyesekere, Gananath.1980. The rebirth eschatology and its transformations: a contribution to the sociology of early Buddhism. IN Karma and rebirth in classical Indian traditions, edited by Wendy O'Flaherty, pp. 137-164, Berkeley: University of California Press, 1980.

Olson, Alan M. 1980. ed. Myth, Symbol, and Reality. Notre Dame, Ind.: University of Notre Dame Press.

Palsule, Gajanan B., 1961. The Sanskrit Dhātupāthas: A Critical Study. Deccan College Dissertation Series, no. 23. Poona: Deccan College.

Pappu, Rama Rao ed. 1987. The dimensions of karma. Delhi: Chanakya Publications.

Parsons, Talcott. 1979. Definitions of Health and Illness in the Light of American Values and Social Structures. In E. G. Jaco (ed)

Patients, Physicians and Illness, 120-144. 1958 reprint. New York: Free Press.

Patanjal, D.P. 1963. A Critical Study of Ṛgveda [1:137-163] Particularly from the Point of View of Paninian Grammar. New Delhi: Patanjal Publishing.

Pelerino, Edmund.1979. Toward a Reconstruction of Medical Morality: The Primacy of Profession and the Fact of Illness. Journal of Medicine & Philosophy 4 (1979): 32-56.

Prasad, Mantrini. 1975. Language of the Nirukta. Delhi: D. K. Publishing House.

Ramanujan, A. K.1990. Is there an Indian way of thinking? In India through Hindu categories, edited by McKim Marriott, pp. 41-58. New Delhi: Sage Publications.

Rayan, Krishna. 1972. Suggestion and Statement in Poetry, London: The Athalone Press.

Ricoeur, Paul. 1992. Oneself as Another, translated by Kathleen Blamey, Chicago: The University of Chicago Press. OA

Scholes, Robert, 1982. Semiotics and interpretation. New Haven: Yale University Press.

Sharma, P. V. 1972. Indian Medicine in the Classical Age. Chowkhamba Sanskrit Series, vol. 85. Varanasi: Chowkhamba.

Shelp, Earl E. (ed) 1985. Virtue and Medicine: Explorations in the Character of Medicine. Dordrecht, Holland: D. Reidel & Co.

Shotter, John Action, joint action and intentionality. 1980. In Brenner, Michael, ed. The structure of action, 25-80, New York: St. Martin's Press.

Smolicz, J. J. 1981. Core Values and Cultural Identity. Ethnic & Social Studies, 4, 75-90

Spicker, Stuart F. and H.Tristam Engelhardt. 1977. Philosophical Medical Ethics: Its Nature & Significance. Proceedings of the Third Trans-disciplinary Symposium on Philosophy & Medicine. Philosophy & Medicine Series edited by Stuart S.

Spicker & H. Tristam Engelhardt vol.3. Dordrecht-Holland: D. Reidel Publishing Co.

Spicker, Stuart F. and H. Tristam Engelhardt.1985. The Virtuous Physician, and the Ethics of Medicine. In Earl E. Shelp (ed) Virtue and Medicine: Explorations in the Character of Medicine. Edited by Earl E. Shelp, 237-255. Dordrecht, Holland: D. Reidel & Co.

Szasz, Thomas. 1985. The Theology of Medicine. New York: Harper Books.

Tilak, Shrinivas.1984. Myth of Sarvodaya: A Study of Vinoba's Concept, New Delhi: Breakthrough Communications.

Tilak, Shrinivas.1989. Religion and Aging in the Indian Tradition, Albany, New York: State University of New York Press.

Tilak, Shrinivas.1992. Interpreting Social Action as Text: A Hindu Perspective. Contributions to Indian Sociology (n.s.), vol 26, no 1 (1992): 151-157.

Tilak, Shrinivas.1994. The Mīmāmsā Theory of Text Interpretation. In Hermeneutical Paths to the Sacred Worlds of India. Edited by Katherine K. Young. 138-59. Atlanta, Ga.: Scholars Press.

Tilak, Shrinivas.1996. Under the Canopy of Tirtha: Patterns of Sharing Sacred Space the Hindu Way. Ecumenism, vol 36, no. 123 (Sept 1996): 12-16.

Tilak, Shrinivas.2006. Understanding karma in light of Paul Ricoeur's philosophical anthropology and hermeneutics. Nagpur, India: International Centre for Cultural Studies.

Towers, Bernard. 1977. Ethics in Evolution. In Stuart S. Spicker & H. Tristam Engelhardt (eds) Philosophical Medical Ethics: Its Nature & Significance, 155-168. Dordrecht-Holland: D. Reidel Publishing Co.

Trafford, Abigail. 2006. Growing old has serious image problem. The Gazette [Washington Post] Montreal, March 27, 2006, p. D2.

Veatch, Robert M. 1985. Against Virtue: A eontological Critique of Virtue Theory in Medical Ethics. In Earl E. Shelp (ed) Virtue and

Medicine: Explorations in the Character of Medicine. Dordrecht, Holland: D. Reidel & Co.

Vishva Bandhu, 1975. Vedic Textuo-Linguistic Studies. Edited & introduction by K. V. Sarma. Hoshiarpur, India: V. V. Research Institute. Vishveshvarananda Indological Series no 49

Wenger, G Clare. 1989. Support Networks in Old Age: Constructing a Typology. In Growing Old in the Twentieth Century, edited by Margot Jefferys, 167-185, London: Routledge.

Whorf, Benjamin, 1966. Language, Thought and Reality, 1956, reprint, edited with introduction by John D. Caroll, Cambridge, Mass.: Technological Press MIT.

Wickler, Daniel. 1987. Personal Responsibility for Illness. In Donald Van De Veer and Tom Regan (eds) Health Care Ethics: An Introduction, 326-358. Philadelphia: Temple University Press.

Zimmermann, Francis.1987. The Jungle and the Aroma of Meats: An Ecological Theme in Hindu Medicine, Berkeley: University of California Press.

Abbreviations

Ah.sū.	*Aşţāngahŗdayam* Sūtra Sthāna
BC	Buddhacarita
BCE	Before Common Era
BCE	Before Common Era
Ca	Carakasamhitā
Ca ci	Carakasamhitā Cikitsā Sthāna
Ca vi	Carakasamhitā Vimāna Sthāna
Ca.	*Carakasamhitā*
Ca.ci.	" Cikitsā Sthāna
Ca.ind.	" Indrīya Sthāna
Ca.ni	" Nidāna Sthāna
Ca.śā.	" Śārīra Sthāna
Ca.sū.	" Sūtra Sthāna
Ca.vi.	" Vimāna Sthāna
CE	Common Era
SD	Saundarananda
Su.	*Suśrutasamhitā*
Su.ci.	" Cikitsā Sthāna
Su.śā.	" Śārīira Sthāna
Su.sū.	" Sūtra Sthāna

About contributors

Sanjeev Bharani (PhD- Mechanical Engineering) is a Senior Engineer-Development/Research in Global Mining Division, Caterpillar, Inc., Decatur, IL.

Shrinarayan Chandak is a graduate chemical engineer and a consultant. He is a national past president of Maheshwari Mahasabha of North America. He is also the vice-president (Midwest region) of Hindu Swayamsevak Sangh, USA.

Milind Deshpande (PhD) is a Research Scientist and Technical dorector of Center for bio-catalysis and bio-processing at the University of Iowa, Iowa City. He is General Secretary of Hindu Swayamsevak Sangh.

Pukhraj Jain is a metallurgical engineer and retired marketing manager from IBM, USA. He is a scholar of the Gita and Jain philosophy.

Srinivas Kalyanraman is a distinguished economist who was director of the Asian Development Bank. He has published several books including the seven volumes *Saraswati Civilization* (Bangalore: Babasaheb Apte Smarak Samiti 2003).

Vimal Patel (PhD) is a professor of pathology at the Indiana University School of Medicine, Indianapolis. He is a prominent community involved in Hindu education in the USA. He is Director of Health Synergies, The Center forIntergative Health Care, Indianpolis.

Yashwant Pathak (PhD) is Chairman, Department of Pharmaceutical Sciences, Sullivan University, Louisville, KY. He is also Co-ordinator for The International Center for Cultural Studies Nagpur, India, in USA.

Greesh C. Sharma (PhD) is a practicing clinical psychologist in Pennsylvania. His latest book, *Thriving in the Unknown: Adventures of a Psychologist* is nearing completion. E-mail <gsc42ol@yahoo.com> Phone (215) 295-3099

Shrinivas Tilak (PhD, McGill) is an independent researcher based in Montreal. His publications include *The Myth of Sarvodaya: A study of Vinoba's concept* Delhi: Breakthrough Communications, 1985), *Religion and Aging in the Indian Tradition* (Albany, N.Y.: State university of New

York Press, 1989), and *Understanding karma in light of Paul Ricoeur's philosophical anthropology and hermeneutics* (Nagpur: International Center for Cultural Studies, 2006).

www.ingramcontent.com/pod-product-compliance
Lightning Source LLC
Chambersburg PA
CBHW051836090426
42736CB00011B/1838
* 9 7 8 1 9 3 4 1 9 2 0 1 6 *